D1599041

# Berlin's Housing Revolution
## German Reform in the 1920s

# Architecture and Urban Design, No. 16

## Stephen C. Foster, Series Editor

Associate Professor of Art History
University of Iowa

## Other Titles in This Series

# Berlin's Housing Revolution
## German Reform in the 1920s

by
Ronald Wiedenhoeft

UMI RESEARCH PRESS
Ann Arbor, Michigan

728.0943155
W646

Copyright © 1985, 1971
Ronald Victor Wiedenhoeft
All rights reserved

Produced and distributed by
UMI Research Press
an imprint of
University Microfilms International
A Xerox Information Resources Company
Ann Arbor, Michigan 48106

Library of Congress Cataloging in Publication Data

**Wiedenhoeft, Ronald V.**
  Berlin's housing revolution.

   (Architecture and urban design ; no. 16)
   Revision of thesis (Ph.D.)—Columbia University,
1971.
   Bibliography: p.
   Includes index.
   1. Housing—Berlin (Germany)—History.
2. Housing policy—Berlin (Germany)—History.
3. Berlin (Germany)—Social conditions.
4. Architecture, Domestic—Berlin (Germany)
I. Title.  II. Series.
  HD7339.B4W53  1985      363.5'094341'55        85-16331
  ISBN 0-8357-1705-4 (alk. paper)

*Dedicated to my father, Kurt Wiedenhoeft*

UNIVERSITY LIBRARIES
CARNEGIE-MELLON UNIVERSITY
PITTSBURGH, PENNSYLVANIA 15213

*Gross-Siedlung Britz (Hufeisen Siedlung)*, Berlin-Neukölln, Bruno Taut and Martin Wagner, 1925–26

Three row-houses in the Hufeisen complex, with a family enjoying the intimate contact with nature that was a fundamental key of German housing reform.
(Photo: Arthur Köster. Courtesy Academie der Künste, Berlin)

# Contents

# Illustrations

# Preface

The purpose of this study is to investigate working-class housing, a generally neglected aspect of modern architecture. In the history of twentieth-century architecture too much concentration on matters of form has resulted in neglect of two of the most powerful motivators which determine architectural form: social values and politics. To give a complete picture of the architectural developments of any place in any age, historians must study and evaluate designs not just from formal but also from social and political viewpoints. This is particularly relevant in the case of Germany in the 1920s, when a revolution in housing was the logical and inevitable result of a revolution in social politics.

Berlin in the 1920s was a hotbed of reform activity in both social and architectural realms. As capital of the Reich and leader of Prussia—the powerful state that incorporated large parts of present-day East and West Germany, including Frankfurt, Cologne and Hannover—Berlin held a preeminent position. It was by far the largest city in Germany, with more than four million inhabitants, while its nearest rival, Hamburg, had only about one million. Berlin was the center for all the most important developments—in publishing, legislation, research, building, and a host of other fields—and it was the recipient in the 1920s of a steady stream of new talent and exciting new ideas, as refugees and emigrees poured in from eastern Europe. Mention of the names of Bruno Taut and Walter Gropius as architects active in Berlin in the field of housing should suffice to indicate Berlin's pioneering role in this field. Thus it quickly became apparent to me that careful scrutiny of ideas, applications, and results in Berlin's housing of the 1920s would yield rich treasures.

The first step was to assess the nature of the housing problem—really a severe housing crisis—in Berlin after the First World War. The second was to research the background of German social reform going back to the mid-nineteenth century. The third step was an analysis of the housing projects built in the 1920s, some of which were well known and well represented in publications internationally. My pursuit of the specifics of individual projects and the discovery of distinct similarities demonstrating clear, underlying principles, however, led me to a fourth step: articulation of the social reform but also the *Werkbund*'s *Weissenhof Siedlung* under Mies van der Rohe. The development of a modern cult around the persons of these two men seems particularly unfortunate and distorting when related to the socialistic goals of the German housing revolution, specifically when related to the concept of collectivism, which played such a major role in achieving the transformation. In order to develop what seemed to me a needed focus on substance rather than personalities and to allow important new considerations to emerge, I have chosen not to go over familiar territory but to attempt to view objectively the phenomenon, its social accomplishments, and the means by which it was achieved.

I initially became interested in this subject while on a Fulbright fellowship in Germany. Further opportunities to develop my interest in the city of Berlin came in the form of my master's thesis at the University of Wisconsin and a subsequent year at the Technical and Free Universities of Berlin on fellowship from the German Academic Exchange Service. Then, as a doctoral candidate at Columbia University, I was awarded a summer's research grant for further work in Berlin. In September of 1967 my work on this subject was abruptly truncated by the East German Security Police, who arrested me on suspicion of espionage while I was in the process of photographing housing projects on their side of the infamous Berlin Wall. When, after nine months' investigatory detention and no trial, I was released, I commented in a press conference that perhaps I should switch to some less dangerous field of research, such as Eskimo pots. Nonetheless, the social significance of housing reform continued to fascinate me, and I completed my doctoral studies at Columbia University.

The concern and generous support of professors, students, and administrators of Columbia University during the period of my incarceration were a source of sustenance to my family of which I was able to learn only later. I shall always be grateful not only for this great support but also for the privilege of teaching as a preceptor while working for my doctorate at Columbia. To Professors George R. Collins and Edgard Kaufmann, Jr., I owe a particular debt of gratitude for their example, leadership, and encouragement in my development of a revisionist approach to architectural history. To Maxwell Raab, now United States Ambassador to Italy, I shall always be grateful for his selfless dedication in attaining my timely release from detention in East Berlin, so that no more than one academic year was lost to this special learning experience.

The sources from which I have been able to gather information over the years have been many and varied, particularly in Berlin itself. My sincere thanks go to all the individuals who helped in ways too numerous to list here. I was especially fortunate to be able to gain first-hand insights from concepts which ran as a common thread through all of the projects, whether famous or not. Fortunately, the Germans of the 1920s were characteristically thorough in documenting and publishing their thought processes in numerous professional journals. The track had only to be followed and the ideas synthesized.

One danger was inherent, though, in this process (and another was subsequently to emerge). In feeling myself compelled to go beyond traditional disciplinary boundaries in pursuing concepts of housing reform, I exposed myself to the constant danger of extending my research into other disciplines, and beyond my own competence. The revision of building codes, the design of minimal standards to achive hygienic conditions, the discovery of means to reduce costs and eliminate speculation, and the application of mechanisms necessary to carry out publicly supported workers' housing emerged as important factors deserving careful consideration if the architecture itself was to be understood.

It soon became apparent that historical studies of the housing reform movement, fraternal self-help building organizations, and government programs, while highly desirable, could only be suggested here. The degree and type of government financing, methods for controlling and disbursing funds, and the relationship between fiscal and quality control should all receive more attention. Yet undoubtedly the most striking revelation to me was the overriding importance of a fundamentally new social ethic and of political decisions based upon that ethic. Here was a society not only in the process of inventing a new form of architecture and a new architectural purpose, but a new way of living as well. What at first appeared as a change in degree, revealed itself as a change in kind; housing reform, through the systematic development of formerly merely nascent ideas, transformed itself into housing revolution.

Why Germany in this period and why the focus on Berlin? Surely other countries went through similar crises after the First World War, eliminating or severely restricting the monarchy and pursuing a course of democratization and limited socialization. England, Holland, Sweden, and Switzerland all were active in building progressive workers' housing during the 1920s. Within Germany, the contemporary work of Ernst May in Frankfurt, of Otto Häsler in Celle, of Walter Gropius in Dessau and Karlsruhe, and of an international group of architects under the direction of Mies van der Rohe in Stuttgart-Weissenhof provided interesting and widely publicized parallels to developments in Berlin. Yet, through a special synergy of politics, economics, social dynamism, and a confluence of intellects, Berlin was the city where—qualitatively and quantitatively—the most exciting work was done.

Other notable German achievements of the period have received ample attention elsewhere: most prominently the Bauhaus under Walter Gropius, conversations with Wassili Luckhardt, Hans Scharoun, Ludwig Hilberseimer, Ludwig Mies van der Rohe, and Max Taut, who have all since passed away. I am also grateful for the opportunity of conversing with Mrs. Martin Wagner and for bibliographic materials from Mrs. Walter Curt Behrendt, which have been deposited in Avery Architectural Library. Professor and Mrs. Rudolf Wittkower also helped me by sharing their first-hand experiences of Berlin in the 1920s.

There can be no adequate description of all that my wife Renate has contributed. To her go my deepest thanks for her encouragement, untiring cooperation, and patience. Finally, I wish to acknowledge the important influence of my father, Kurt Wiedenhoeft, an inspiration and ever-confident patron of my endeavors, who gave me my early introduction to the world of construction and housing. It is to him that this book is dedicated.

# 1

# Historical Background

## Workers' Housing: Some Fundamental Considerations

The concept of "workers' housing" can be extremely broad, including the living facilities of all people who earn their living by working with their hands or their minds. Common understanding, however, links the concept to the housing of lower-income groups in cities. What they do to support themselves is not as important a defining factor as their limited ability to pay and, hence, limited ability to seek desirable accomodations on the open market. Workers' housing is thus inevitably linked to less desirable minimal dwellings with greater or lesser degrees of disamenity. In Germany around 1900 it was rare that a working-class dwelling exceeded two or three rooms, sometimes with a separate kitchen, often with no other source of heat than the cooking stove, and usually with only shared toilet facilities outside the dwelling unit. There was no minimum.

Historically, workers' housing had come to imply tiny, squalid quarters in the urban core, with little possibility for good hygiene or well-being among those forced by circumstances to inhabit them. Although all major urban centers in industrialized countries have a history of depressed living conditions for the poor, no European city had worse conditions than Berlin before, during, and just after the First World War. The reverse of the coin, however, gives the subject of this study its great appeal: Berlin's preeminent record of attacking the housing crisis and making major strides in social reform.

## Housing Crisis

A housing crisis exists when the housing supply—in terms of numbers of units, price, and quality—is inadequate to meet the needs and demands of a society. The manifestations of such a crisis are social malaise: imbalance between rents and income, severe overcrowding, bad health statistics, decay, blight, and filth. Inevitably a housing crisis is a crisis of small dwellings and poor people, i.e., a crisis for those who have the least political power and are least well represented.

In the years 1910–14 Werner Hegemann was active in calling attention to the drastic housing situation in Berlin. In 1912 he was publicly denounced for "agitating to stir up class hatred" by planning to publish a poster, eloquently illustrated by Käthe Kollwitz, in which objective facts of the housing situation in Berlin were stated: "In greater Berlin 600,000 people live in apartments in which each room is occupied by five or more persons. Hundreds of thousands of children are without a place to play."[1]

## The Berlin Rental Barracks

Urban planning in Berlin in the second half of the nineteenth century was based upon the French prototype created for Paris under Napoleon III. The layout of broad avenues and streets, with an emphasis on impressive facades, was expensive and brought with it high taxes and heavy exploitation through high-density building, developing the so-called garden areas behind the facades with cramped, oppressive quarters. A period of economic liberalism, the late nineteenth century was characterized by minimal government control or interference. Private initiative and speculators had a free hand in exploiting both land and people.

Following the Franco-Prussian War of 1870–71, Berlin experienced a period of unprecedented expansion. The city planning aspects of this development boom followed the grandiose Parisian schemes slavishly: wide, imposing streets with tall, decorated facades. Maximum use squeezed out of the allowed height caused a continuing spiral with increasing land prices forcing still higher utilization, which in turn drove land even higher. Finally, just before the First World War, the average occupancy per building in Berlin had reached seventy-six people, ten times the density of London and double that of Paris. Inevitably, land was also ten times as expensive in Berlin as it was in London. The differences clearly resulted from different attitudes about what type of house construction should be the norm and from the practice in Berlin of allowing speculators to determine the form taken by urban structures. Physically Berlin could have expanded in all directions; other German cities with higher degrees of industrialization had lower housing densities. But development per se seems to have been considered the highest good in Berlin, and the resulting building type came to be known as the rental barracks *(Mietskaserne):* characteristically a five-story walk-up with pretentiously ornamented facade and middle-class apartments facing the street but side wings and three or four additional buildings of miserably cramped small dwellings at the rear, bringing site coverage up as high as ninety percent. These back tenements, or "garden buildings" (an ironic designation based on the usage for which this land was originally intended) consisted of tiny units clustered three or four to a landing, with inadequate light and ventilation, no baths, and shared water closets (at best) on the landings between stories, or (at worst) outhouses in the courtyard below, where a single toilet was often shared by ten or even more families.

> Between 1853 and 1857 in Berlin, the building code permitted buildings six and a half stories high (although many were higher), sixty-five feet wide and one hundred sixty-five feet deep, covering all of the plot except three inner air shafts, each about seventeen feet square.[2]

While some of these specific figures had been somewhat ameliorated in subsequent decades, squalor seemed only to increase. One of the many comments on the unbearable housing conditions prevalent in Berlin is provided in a little booklet entitled *Fifty Years' Battle Against the Rental Barracks,* in which the history of these oppressive quarters is summarized:

> The galloping industrial development of Germany in the last decades of the nineteenth century led to a concentration of people in cities. Upon this fact was founded a growing exploitation of land that led to an endless climb in its cost and an increasingly dense building-up of sites. The number of stories increased; the surface area of courtyards steadily decreased; the rental barracks were born. These conditions were particularly severe in the capital of the Reich.[3]

"Back to the Land!" was one solution called for by many housing reformers over the years. Reflecting this view, on March 26, 1917, the Prussian Minister of Public Works, Paul von Breitenbach, published a series of guidelines for the encouragement of low-density housing developments on the periphery of the cities, commenting in his introduction how critically bad housing conditions—particularly in Berlin—had become:

> The retrogressive development in the population growth which has been observed for years and which has become increasingly important because of the heavy losses in the war, makes it the serious duty of the national government to encourage all appropriate means to counteract the difficulties that stand in the way of maintaining and raising large families in the cities.... Unprecedented steps will have to be taken to relocate portions of the urban population into small houses with gardens or attached land on the periphery or in the near vicinity of the cities.[4]

Conditions were not only oppressive but "hellish," as many commentators reported, with a decreasing birth rate, high numbers of abortions, high infant mortality, and widespread rickets and tuberculosis. Returning the working class to life-giving contact with the earth—to nature as the prime source of energy and strength—was seen as an essential step toward human regeneration.

Yet the building of such small settlements dispersed across the landscape could not be attractive to commercial builders, nor could low-density settlements be offered at affordable prices or rental rates if built commercially. This point had been emphasized by one of the developers prominent in speculative housing in Berlin, Georg Haberland, of the Berlinische Bodengesellschaft. Haberland, who bore the distinguished title of *Kommerzienrat* in recognition of his pre-war development of large tracts of Berlin land with *Mietskasernen,* advocated such large, high-density housing developments as the best means to "social and cultural improvement." Naturally, he was despised by socially-minded architects and housing reformers. In 1919, Martin Wagner, a key figure about whom we will have more to say, publicly criticized Haberland's twisting of words to make the speculators' best interests appear identical with those of the people. In attacking Haberland, Wagner expressed the social goal of architects and planners whose plan was to save the vitality of the German nation by helping people escape from the rental barracks.[5]

The year 1919 was significant in providing new laws governing the use of the land, laws which provided a foundation for the housing settlements of the 1920s. Their fundamental purpose, and also that of Articles 153 and 155 of the Constitution of the Republic, was to enable the government to acquire and control land, removing it from the grasp of speculators. All of this was based on the concept that possession of land does not entitle the possessor to unlimited exploitation, but rather demands certain responsibilities of him. "Possession creates responsibility: use of the land must serve the common good" is the fundamental statement of this ethical principle in Article 153 of the Weimar Constitution. The social ethic stated in this one sentence represents an about-face from the principles that had governed housing and development in Berlin before 1914.

The means chosen to assure the responsible use of land was municipal ownership or control of large tracts of land in and around cities. Land owned by the community could be leased out at very low interest rates as a form of direct influence and subsidy for desirable low-cost housing. Offering of government land for lease was also an indirect means of influencing prices of land held by the private sector. Municipal influence or control could also be exerted through restrictive zoning and other city planning measures. The use of forceful planning to place the best interests of the community as a whole above private profit was a crucial early stage of the German housing revolution.

Yet another crucial stage—as important as controlling the availability of low-cost land—was achieving an impact on the cost of money. Somehow, if low-cost housing for the masses was to become available, means of reducing interest rates had to be found. One way was to turn over construction to limited dividend, public benefit building corporations. Another way was to offer direct subsidies or building loans at low rates with long periods of amortization. Direct government control over the source of money also afforded an opportunity of controlling quality in housing approved for state loans. All of these measures were applied in the 1920s; in Berlin policies of municipal control of the land and city or state-administered low-cost financing were effectively applied. Cheap land and cheap money were essential elements in mounting a campaign to provide adequate shelter for the masses. The collapse of the program in 1931 became inevitable when the means for government support finally disappeared.

**Early Development of City Planning**

1874 marked the fiftieth anniversary of the Berlin Architects' Association *(Architekten Verein zu Berlin)* and the first congress of the Federated Associations of German Architects and Engineers *(Verband Deutscher Architekten- und Ingenieur-Vereine).* In Berlin at that joint celebration Reinhard Baumeister took what might be considered the first significant step in the direction of establishing a new discipline of city planning. It was the year of his first book on the subject, *Fundamentals of Urban Expansion (Gundzüge für Stadterweiterungen),* and he drew the attention of the assembled architects to the need for considering broader issues than merely designing streets and buildings. In 1876 he published a further development of his ideas as *Urban Expansion: Technical, Political, and Economic Aspects (Stadterweiterungen in technischer, baupolitscher und wirtschaftlicher Beziehung),* in which he gave particular attention to problems of housing and urban hygiene. Thus it is from the mid-1870s that one can date the systematic development of a professional approach to solving urban development problems. Yet it was not until after the First World War that large scale solutions to problems caused by misguided development were attempted.

City planning in the nineteenth century continued to be a matter of esthetics. Along with Baron Haussmann's designs for the *grands boulevards* in Paris in the 1850s, major attention was focused on Vienna, its competition designs (1858) and subsequently the development of the monumental Ringstrasse in the broad band of what formerly had been urban fortifications. Characteristic for this period is the lack in all of these programs of proposals to improve or transform urban housing. Instead, all attention seems to have been concentrated on creating imposing effects in public spaces. The efficient and productive interrelationships of all types of land use in cities seems not to have been recognized as an important design concern, although certainly Baumeister was showing the way.

Competitions for urban expansion plans for Strassburg in 1879 and

Cologne in 1880 served to stimulate an awareness in Germany that problems other than the esthetic needed to be considered in urban design. Joseph Stübben, who ten years later was to publish the first edition of his influential book on city planning *(Der Städtebau),* was the winner of the Cologne competition and became a leader in the young discipline. Yet his designs were still characterized by monumental boulevards and radiating-star intersections of the Parisian type.

In the same decade the Austrian Camillo Sitte provided a great new impetus with the publication, in 1889, of his book on *City Planning According to Artistic Principles (Der Städte-Bau nach seinen künstlerischen Grundsätzen).* His technique of analyzing historic urban spaces in Europe and showing how a psychologically satisfying quality of containment and of outdoor urban rooms could be achieved through design was a startling revelation which carried a ring of truth. These concepts were accepted so readily that Sitte's influence spread quite rapidly, finally bringing about the discrediting of the star-intersection-and-grand-boulevard school of planning. The shift in thinking was so substantial that Sitte has been given credit for the birth of modern city planning.[6] Yet as important and salutory as Sitte's concepts were, they still dealt with esthetic matters and had little to offer concerning housing reform or ways to improve the living conditions of the masses.

The books by Baumeister, Stübben, and Sitte loosed a flood of technical and esthetic studies concerning various aspects of urban design. Such details as the merits of open versus closed street fronts, curved versus straight streets, open versus closed squares or vistas, the arrangement and breaking of building lines, design and location of public parks, appropriate public transit systems, and so on were extensively debated in the decades bracketing the turn of the century. Meanwhile, the country-to-city migration continued in force, and the problem of suitable housing for the masses was left unaddressed by the city planning specialists.

While administrators and planners devoted their attention to other matters, the most pressing urban problems continued to be housing, housing, housing, and the dreadful conditions steadily worsened in the decades leading up to the war, becoming truly oppressive when the war brought about a nearly complete halt to new housing construction. Virtually unscrutinized and unregulated by public authority, workers' housing in the industrial centers was a festering wound, causing alienation, anomie, and dire health problems. While socially conscious reformers repeatedly warned of the serious consequences of neglecting this social timebomb, administrators and legislators did nothing to alleviate the situation.

With the conspicuous exceptions of small self-help building cooperatives and paternalistic projects for municipal employees or company housing—

such as the settlements for workers at the Krupp concern in Essen—housing for workers during the Wilhelmine period presented a dismal picture. It was not seen as the social responsibility it was to become in the twenties, but remained a step-child of the land developers and unscrupulous contractors. Scandalously shoddy, exploitative, and frequently fraudulant building practices were not only tolerated by officialdom but supported by police power when occasional mini-revolts broke out. The great watershed in attitudes was the November Revolution of 1918, after which social responsibility and public welfare became official policy.

Social democracy—while not the exclusive domain of the Social Democratic Party (SPD)—is an appropriate designation for this growing spirit of change. The mutiny of sailors in Kiel in the first days of November began the flash fire of revolution across the country, in which the Soldiers' and Workers' Councils *(Soldaten- und Arbeiterräte)* seized power from military and civilian authorities. In Berlin on the climactic day of November 9, 1918, Philipp Scheidemann proclaimed the republic, Karl Liebknecht proclaimed Germany a socialist republic, the Kaiser abdicated, the Crown Prince disclaimed his right to succession, and Prince Max von Baden turned over his authority as Chancellor of the Reich to Social Democrat Friedrich Ebert. The era of social reform—if not of thorough socialization, as many wished—had begun.

On February 11, 1919, Ebert was elected president of the republic. Social reform—in particular efforts to solve the housing crisis—was a matter of government policy. The politics of reform were destined to have a profound influence on the provision, distribution, and design of housing.

## Housing Reform

Housing reform has the potential for great impact in modern city planning. While housing as a problem for the majority of people has been a constant theme throughout history, severe housing problems are particularly characteristic of the era of industrialization. Since expansion of industry requires great numbers of workers concentrated in urban centers, major shifts in population from the countryside into the cities are inevitable corollaries. Since low-skilled, poorly paid industrial workers, however, do not form an attractive market for developers, historically they have had to make do with unappealing, substandard dwellings ranging in quality from poor to dismal. Without government intervention, mechanisms of the free market are unlikely to alleviate a downward spiral of housing deprivation, social malaise, and workers' inability to improve their position in society. The tragic effects spread from individuals and families to neighborhoods and communities, and ultimately can debilitate entire nations.

Early steps toward housing reform in Germany are usually dated from an 1840 report by Victor Aimé Huber on pathetic living conditions among workers.[7] Gradually organizations with such names as Association for Social Politics *(Verein für Sozialpolitik)* and German Association for the Advancement of Health *(Deutscher Verein für Gesundheitspflege)* concerned themselves with gathering data and publicizing bad housing conditions among the poor. Their propaganda and agitation were aimed at one primary goal: legislation for housing reform. Among their fundamental demands was the removal of workers' housing from the grasp of private exploiters and speculators. They felt that, since the well- or ill-being of the nation depended so directly on the type and quality of housing generally available, this particular aspect of the national economy should be removed from the free market that had failed so miserably and instead be treated as a public service.

Since cities were perceived as the breeding grounds of virtually all evil, decentralization was also an integral part of the striving toward housing reform. Various plans were proposed for transferring groups of underprivileged city dwellers to dispersed, idyllic settlements in the country, and concepts of "inner colonization," "back to the land," and the dispersal of industry throughout the country were fundamental to reform movements through the Wilhelmine Second Reich and the Weimar Republic, and on into Hitler's Third Reich as well.

## The Land Reform Movement

Essential to the concept of low-density, anti-urban settlements is the political idea of land reform, which derives from the conviction that land is such a basic resource that using it should be as much a human right as breathing air or drinking water. Instead of allowing anyone to exercise control over this basic resource, land was to belong to society in its totality.[8] No earned profit increment should be allowed to accrue to individuals, it was felt, since any increase in land value should benefit the community and enrich everyone. Furthermore, the best interests of the community rather than the profit motive should dictate how land is used, a concept essential to establishing and retaining modest population densities anywhere. As opposed to Marxist expropriation and collectivization, however, the view that came to dominate the German land reform movement was that selective taxes on land should be imposed to prevent speculation.

The leading figure in German land reform was Adolf Damaschke, a Social Democrat, teacher, and writer. In 1891 he became leader of the German Association for Land Reform *(Deutscher Bund für Bodenreform)*, yet in 1898 he reported that there were still only "140 kindred spirits in the entire German-language area." Damaschke reorganized the group as the *Bund Deutscher*

*Bodenreformer* in that year and had doubled its membership to 290 by 1899. Tireless and effective in propagating the cause, in 1902 Damaschke published his major work, *Land Reform: A Fundamental and Historical Approach toward Recognition and Relief of the Social Crisis.*[9] It was highly regarded by leaders of the German Socialist movement and received surprisingly broad endorsement from many sections of society.

From 1898 on, German land reformers de-emphasized the radical concept of communal ownership of all land and all housing in favor of action programs to improve housing conditions among the working class. Lobbying to achieve favorable legislation was one of the most valuable contributions of Damaschke and his followers. Among their goals were establishment of publicly funded mortgages at low interest rates, the retention and expansion of publicly owned land to be made available for housing construction, legislation against speculative exploitation, and public programs of "inner colonization"; in other words, a series of goals which came to be realized in the housing revolution of the 1920s.

The war and consequent cessation of building activity brought about a great improvement in attitudes toward housing and land reform. Damaschke initiated a veterans' homestead movement *(Kriegerheimstättenbewegung),* which received widespread public support. If for no other than political reasons, public officials including Field Marshal von Hindenburg lent verbal support to Damaschke's proposal to provide 500,000 returning soldiers with their own homes and pieces of the homeland to till. In retrospect some felt that, had it been possible to realize this scheme, the revolution of 1918 could have been defused. Because of the dire housing shortage at the time, many of the soldiers released from the front at the cessation of hostilities could return to no home at all. They were left quite literally on the streets to form a discontented and potent political force.

The hope for veterans' homesteads did not die. Instead, this concept became basic to the new republic's campaign against the housing crisis. The most immediate beneficiary of new housing legislation just after the war was the homestead movement. Summarizing the "back-to-the-soil" spirit of land reform, Leberecht Migge in 1919 wrote, "There is no longer any doubt: an elevated and harmonious human life cannot be conceived without a relationship to the earth."[10]

Sociopolitical reform was also essential to progressive housing in the 1920s. Planners and reformers alone could have achieved nothing. All concepts of using land for healthful settlements were dependent upon community control of the land and public financing at low interest rates, both of which depended upon strong political action. Without these, advanced, inexpensive housing for low-income groups could not have been built. The fact that many exemplary projects were indeed built in Germany during the

1920s—despite extreme financial handicaps—demonstrates the success of the pioneering reformers as well as the success of socially minded politicians of the Weimar Republic.

## The Garden Cities Movement

An important predecessor to the housing revolution of the 1920s was the garden cities movement, in Germany as well as in England and the Netherlands. This influential idea was, in fact, a plan for the social reform of workers' housing, which involved relieving overcrowded urban centers by building self-sufficient, free-standing new communities well away from the cities. Reforming housing conditions, providing a supportive environment for fulfilling work, and encouraging subsistence gardening were all key elements in the program. Also fundamental to the idea of garden cities was communal posession of the land in perpetuity, with all increase in value accruing to the group as a whole rather than to individuals.[11]

The first German plan for such an ideal city of the future, employing basic garden city concepts of land reform and organization, was published by Theodor Fritsch as *The City of the Future (Die Stadt der Zukunft)* in 1896. While Fritsch's book did not generate a major movement in Germany, *Tomorrow, a Peaceful Path to Real Reform,* the book of the Englishman Ebenezer Howard two years later, did. Howard's concepts, similar to but developed independently of Fritsch's, generated a genuine garden city movement and visible results in England. The British movement and the example of the Garden City Letchworth—built under the direction of Raymond Unwin—had great influence in Germany and resulted in the founding of the German Garden City Society *(Deutsche Gartenstadt Gesellschaft)* in 1902. Its leaders were Bernhard and Hans Kampffmeyer, Franz Oppenheimer, and A. Otto. In the pages of their periodical, *Gartenstadt,* which began being published in 1906, great attention was devoted to reporting developments in England, and annual tours to see these first-hand were organized as well. Raymond Unwin contributed to the periodical, and, from 1920 on, his *City Planning in Practice* (translated as *Grundlagen des Städtebaues*) was a standard reference work for German architects and planners.

One basic aspect of the garden city concept was the incorporation of decentralized industry to make the community economically independent. Although realized in England, this was not achieved in Germany; consequently, developments there were technically garden suburbs rather than garden cities. (Some so-called garden cities in Germany and elsewhere were simply commercial developments using a pleasant-sounding name and had nothing to do with the movement.) But the concept of homesteads—an important component of garden cities—was quite widely realized in post-war Germany. Be it ever so humble, a homestead—a house with a piece of land to till—was considered the most effective means of saving German workers from physical and moral degeneration.

## Legislation to Encourage Settlements

All the striving of two generations of visionary reformers culminated in legislation achieved in Prussia shortly before and immediately after the end of the First World War, especially the Prussian Housing Law of March 28, 1918. Among its many provisions was government support for non-profit building cooperatives. A Mortgage Security Law of April 10, 1918 set up a system whereby the state would guarantee mortgages as a means of encouraging the construction of inexpensive small houses and apartments. A State Commission for Housing was established for Prussia on May 17, 1918, and for the Reich on August 31, 1918.

On January 15, 1919, an ordinance concerning lease-hold building rights and establishing practices for leasing government-owned land gave unprecedented encouragement for inexpensive small housing in low-density settlements. The Weimar Constitution of August 11, 1919 incorporated into Article 155 a statement of principle formulated by Adolf Damaschke asserting the fundamental right of every German to decent housing. Also in Article 155 the state accepted the responsibility for supervising the use of land and stimulating construction of adequate housing for all, with priority given to large families and veterans. The power of expropriation to further these ends was specifically granted. Article 10 of the Constitution gave the government broad powers to control land use, land distribution, and programs for housing and homesteads. It is significant that a Settlement Law *(Reichssied-lungsgesetz)* was passed on the same day as the Weimar Constitution. It stressed the importance of settlements on undeveloped land as a means of reducing the burdens on the cities and simultaneously of bringing new life to the countryside. Finally, the Homestead Law of May 10, 1920 made further provisions for expropriation, division, and distribution of large landholdings, such as the domains of the Junkers.[12]

The concepts incorporated in this legislation were not new. New and unprecedented in Germany was the fact that such ideas for reforming housing and living conditions had become matters of official policy and public law. It is interesting to note that the Association for Housing Reform had originally called itself the Association for Housing Legislation. The highest priority of reformers—obtaining legislation—finally had been achieved.

**The Concept of Settlement**

*Siedlung* may be effectively translated into English as "settlement." In German, as in English, a settlement is a community with a certain degree of planned cohesion, implying harmonious interaction among its members. On the other hand, simply taking possession of the land, establishing a fixed dwelling upon it, and making one's living from it are also activities associated with settlement or *Siedlung*. The person who engages in such activities is called a settler or *Siedler,* words which in both languages imply tilling the soil. This duality is fundamental to the 1920s *Seidlungen:* unified communities and an intimate relationship to the land. A *Siedlung* is not simply a housing project, but rather group housing ideally designed as a community and with a close and fruitful relationship to the land. There was always an implication— at least in the early years—that a degree of subsistence gardening was needed in order to achieve physical and moral regeneration from the debased state to which urban workers had sunk.

The focus of this book is on settlements within Greater Berlin, and, as we shall see, these consisted of single-family houses (sometimes detached or semi-detached, but more frequently attached as row houses), each with its own subsistence garden; large settlements *(Gross-Siedlungen),* consisting of row houses (with gardens) or apartments (usually without gardens, but often with the possibility of allotment gardens nearby); a combination of the two, often with a certain amount of unified open space; and finally urban housing *(Wohnbauten)* of various advanced types, incorporating light, air, sunshine, and greenery into the design of low-rent housing for the working class in the city. What we shall refer to here as apartments might better be called four-family or eight-family row houses, since—like the one-family row houses— they were only two rooms deep, with only two units per stair landing, thus giving each family open exposure on both sides of the building.

Whereas *Gross-Siedlung* clearly implied a large number of units, there was also the implication that there would be some communal facilities—at least meeting rooms, perhaps shops, playgrounds, or communal laundries— which would help stimulate the feeling of belonging to a group. All three of the major types were expressions of a desire to achieve reduced density and decentralization of urban workers' housing, decentralization which, had it been carried to its logical conclusion, would have meant the dissolution of the cities.

# 2

# Dissolution and New Building

## The Dissolution of Cities: The Book

*The Dissolution of Cities*, as promulgated by Bruno Taut in his book of that name *(Die Auflösung der Städte)*, is usually seen as an expression of utopian fantasy.[1] However, despite the fanciful appearance of the book, the dissolution of cities was considered at the time to be a serious element of programs for social betterment through housing reform. Bruno Taut was not only an inspired and inspiring visionary, but was to become one of Berlin's leaders in building workers' housing. "Let them collapse, those constructed meannesses, " he said of the brutal urban rental barracks (fig. 1). "Stone houses make stone hearts," wrote Taut, quoting an old Russian proverb. "Stone" was used with the same connotation by Werner Hegemann later in his book *The Stone Berlin: a History of the World's Largest Rental-Barracks City.*[2]

Dissolution in this sense expressed a revolutionary desire to destroy the old order. For architects it was the old order as manifested in the established system of housing: so dense, so crowded as to seem more of stone than of space: "constructed meannesses." A popular expression of the time was "You can kill a person as well with a dwelling as with an ax." The dissolution of the cities called for by Taut and others meant primarily the dissolution of the imprisoning urban housing conditions best exemplified by Berlin.

> Within the communist ideology by which we are sustained, the battle-cry is "freedom for Mankind!" The dissolution necessary to accomplish this is a transitional stage. Therefore we ignore this condition in our artistic aspirations and live fully in the freest fantasies, in order to contribute to the coming spirit of our age an architecture, if not indeed art itself.[3]

The above was written by Hans Luckhardt at exactly the same time that Bruno Taut was drawing up *Ausflösung*, his utopian "parable about the third millenium" (fig. 2). Luckhardt's statement helps relate "dissolution" to the

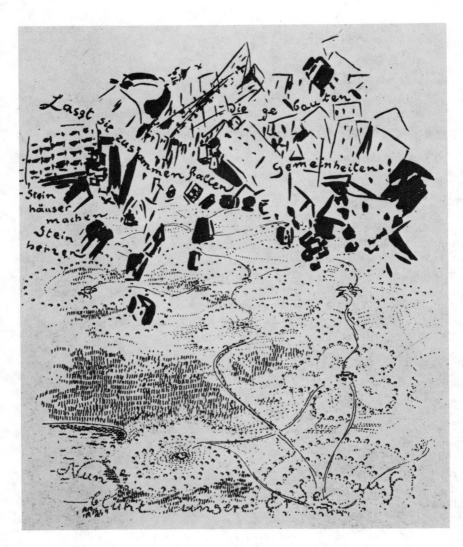

Figure 1.   Bruno Taut put an artist's curse on the overcrowded, unsanitary, antisocial living
            conditions in the speculative rental barracks of the big cities such as Berlin. "Let
            them collapse, those constructed meannesses," he said, and complained that
            houses of stone (meaning the rental barracks) were turning peoples' hearts to
            stone. The ideal alternative he envisioned consisted of various kinds of garden
            settlements for workers dispersed throughout the countryside. "Now our land can
            blossom forth."
            (Taut, *Die Auflösung der Städte,* plate 1)

idealistic aspirations and communist inspirations of Taut's circle. Behind the seemingly free fancy of their forms lay a precicely delineated program of social reform.

Within such a program, dissolution had another connotation: decentralization. In striving to overcome the evils of cities, the possibility for salvation was seen in utopian settlements scattered across the land. *Siedlungen,* drawing life-giving sustenance directly from Nature, were seen as the ideal toward which to aspire.

> The huge spiders—the cities—are only remembrances of a past era, as are the states. City and state, one along with the other, are dead. In place of "the fatherland" has come "homeland" *(die Heimat).* And everyone can find a home anywhere, if he works. There is no more city and country, and no more war and peace. No longer do those abstractions hold power over life, work, happiness, and health. Rather, out of a natural relationship of activity and life, common interests develop which lead to creating institutions for shelter, exchange, education, and further development.[4]

Supporting this impassioned argument for decentralization to improve man's social state, Taut quoted Jean-Jacques Rousseau, saying that "people are not made to swarm in anthills, but rather to spread out over the land, which they should cultivate."[5]

We should not be hasty in dismissing such rhetoric as a misguided vision of returning to an agrarian society. It was utopian and fantastic, perhaps, but more practicable and carefully thought out than would first appear. Taut conceived two distinct types of settlement, which he felt would work together in a spirit of mutual help, the agricultural cooperative *(Landarbeitsgemein-schaft),* and the industrial cooperative *(Arbeitsgemeinschaft)* which would include small and medium-sized plants and shops. The existence of the manufacturing communities was fundamental to the idea of decentralization, and many people would continue to earn their livelihood through industry. Communal ideals dictated that manufacturers would assist the neighboring agriculturalists at harvest time, and of course, "everywhere man must have the expanse of earth that he needs by reason of his nature."[6]

The degree to which Taut recognized practical realities is demonstrated by his inclusion of heavy industry in his scheme—"necessary work-centers, wharves, foundaries, mines, and such." In short, urban centers were to remain for certain purposes, but only heavy industry was essential to such centers. Every other aspect of manufacturing was to be conducted in decentralized communities in direct contact with nature. There would be denser settlements near the "stem" of heavy industry, but radiating "branches" of lesser density would reach out toward the cooperative communities in the countryside.

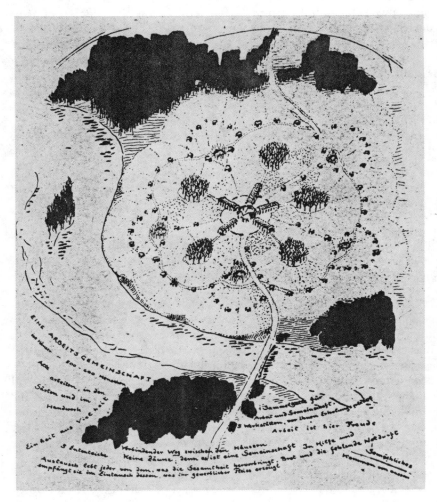

Figure 2.  The ideal workers' commune envisioned by reformers after the war was well
articulated by Taut. This summarizes the prototype for low-density workers'
settlements built in Berlin in the 1920s: "100 houses. 500 to 600 people. All work
in gardens as well as various crafts. Unity in multiplicity. A communal hall for
work and community activities. Five workshops with connected areas for
recreation. Work here is pleasure. Paths link the houses. Five duckponds, no
fences, since this is a cooperative community. In mutual help and cooperation,
everyone lives from the total production of the group. Bread and other missing
necessities are obtained through exchange for products of their diligence."
(Taut, *Auflösung,* plate 2)

### The Dissolution of Cities: The Reality

Thus it becomes clear that an important prerequisite to achieving the ideal relationship of the people to the land in a natural system with settlements "blossoming" across the countryside was the decentralization of industry. Combining the decentralization of manufacturing (*Werkstattaussiedlung*— workshop relocation) with the benefits of decentralized housing for workers was considered by many to be the ultimate goal for future development. It was part of the striving toward socialism that characterized important segments of Weimar society, particularly in the early post-war years.

One of the many factors preventing such a dissolution of cities was the irresistible countertrend in industry of centralizing operations in large plants in or near the major urban centers, especially Berlin. Under the nation's first working-class president, Friedrich Ebert, large cities were seen as a reality that had to be accepted. *Auflösung* in practice became *Auflockerung,* a loosening rather than a dissolving of cities.

This "loosening" or reduction of density was aided in Berlin by the relocation of major industries beyond the periphery of the previously urbanized areas. The heavy machinery and electrical industries were particularly involved, as exemplified by the world-famous firms of Borsig and Siemens & Halske. In the late nineteenth century, these companies had moved northwest and north to the Berlin suburbs of Moabit and Wedding. By 1920 these areas were no longer suburbs but overcrowded, low-class workers' slums, and this reputation clings to them (although with far less justification) to the present day. Moabit and Wedding, though, were not out far enough to become the nuclei of freestanding, independent communities.

In the twenties, these factories moved further north and west toward the more distant communities of Tegel and Spandau, but still Berlin grew out to meet them, although this time large parcels of intervening land were preserved for parks, gardens and low-density development. Much of the new building of workers' settlements in the twenties was directly related to the relocation of such firms as Borsig and Siemens to undeveloped land on the urban fringes. While a far cry from the dissolution or decentralization ideally envisioned, these relocations did provide important opportunities to build impressive new communities of workers' dwellings. It is perhaps ironic that the famous settlements at Britz, Zehlendorf and Siemensstadt may have helped prevent the realization of true garden cities or satellite towns in Germany.

By opting to move to the periphery of the large city, industry diverted energy and pressure away from the development of a truly decentralized system. Instead, a compromise solution was pursued: low-density, outlying garden settlements, each with its own village character. Design efforts were concentrated on developing communities of *Volkswohnungen,* dwellings for the common man. These were related to the established urban pattern and were closely linked to it by the continually expanding rapid transit system.

### *Die Volkswohnung:* Dwellings for the Common Man

The decade 1920–30 began with a concentration on helping the common man into a decent place to live: small, simple and inexpensive, but above all healthy and supportive of family life. As one might expect in the parlance of a German social revolution, such a dwelling, this worthy social goal, was dubbed the People's Dwelling, *die Volkswohnung.*

As we have seen, the brutalizing aspects of the typically wretched quarters for workers in Berlin brought forth a strong opposing reaction, leading everyone to conclude that the revolutionary solution would have to include restored contact with nature. *Die Volkswohnung* then was not only to be small and extremely economical, but to be built on rural or semi-rural land, with low infrastructure costs, and every encouragement was to be given to subsistence agriculture as a new and important element in the lives of urban workers.

Other important concerns in developing the reform concepts of people's dwellings included the means to encourage social interaction, access to goods and services, public transit links to the city, and especially inexpensive and efficient techniques of construction. One key periodical devoted to these issues was *Die Volkswohnung,* subtitled *Periodical for Housing Construction and Settlements.* It was published from 1919 to 1925 under the editorial guidance of Walter Curt Behrendt, who also served as a consultant on housing and planning to the Prussian Ministry of Public Works, Health, and Finance.

In his introductory remarks, Behrendt gave the current estimate of the housing deficit in Germany as 750,000–800,000 units and dedicated the periodical to stimulating construction and providing technical advice for the planning, financing, and building of *Siedlungen.* In a time of severe economic austerity and acute housing shortages, great care had to be taken to maintain high standards of design and technical efficiency. The tone of *Die Volkswohnung* was characterized by an emphasis on socialism and a dedication to practical reform, including the socialization of all and sundry aspects of housing, among them, the building trades, public support for housing, house ownership, and even household goods.

These topics reveal the revolutionary spirit of the times and of the men who were to be leading forces in planning and building when things got under way in 1924 following the great, debilitating inflation. Many of the radical goals of socialism were not to be realized, yet many well known architects struggled long and hard in the vanguard of the fight to reform society. *Die Volkswohnung* documents some of these struggles.

In the summer of 1918 Bruno Taut developed his concept of utopia in terms of the earth as a good dwelling and published "Die Erde eine gute Wohnung" in *Die Volkswohnung* in February of 1919. In this article, besides revealing some of his utopian political concepts regarding anarchism and distribution of the land, Taut described the difficulties encountered in Germany in realizing socialism as he and his compatriots envisioned it:

> In the first days of the revolution people spoke of the fact that now the land would be made free, that large land holdings would be expropriated and divided into small farms and gardens freely distributed. On these the people could return to Mother Earth. But what happened? Endless disputations in meetings and newspapers concerning the pro and con of the theories, and not a single step toward realization. Why such cowardice? Did they think that every step in that direction would be a deathblow to the heart of the city? And that the first step would have been taken toward breaking up the city and transforming our entire culture? The socialistic papers cry, "Workers! Get out of the mass graves of the cities!" But how? Where is the program for settling the land? . . . In the great French Revolution in 1792 the fulfillment of Rousseau's demands appeared to all as a golden hope. Today we have come but a few steps further. Our revolution let the same hope flare up again. After 126 years is this hope to be just as much in vain?[7]

Without going any further into an analysis of the writings of Bruno Taut,[8] it is nevertheless clear that he spoke the language of the time and saw the concepts of planned decentralization and *Siedlung* as political expressions. Architects' contributions to socialization—*Kleinhaus, Kleingarten,* and *Kleinsiedlung*— were the means whereby the working man was to re-establish contact with nature, with himself, and with life. This was Taut's goal; this was Behrendt's goal; this was the goal of *Die Volkswohnung* and seemingly of all its contributors. Yet it requires careful reading to perceive the idealism. On the surface the journal appears to be nothing but dry practicality clothed in sparse, economical forms, advocating the use of the cheapest materials possible.

By contrast, Bruno Taut's book, *The Dissolution of Cities*—for which he used *Die Erde eine gute Wohnung* as a subtitle—might appear to be pure, visionary fantasy. But both Taut's book and his article spoke clearly in practical as well as visionary terms. Both referred to the benefits of a simple country life and to a vision of decentralized settlements blossoming across the landscape. Taut even mentioned the possibility of using tamped earth for building houses, an example of his sincere search for economy in construction.[9] He was not alone. Building techniques employing clay, straw and other inexpensive materials were studied and thoroughly reported in the pages of *Die Volkswohnung,* and the technique of building with tamped earth or clay was the subject of the first supplementary study published by this journal.

The history of progressive architecture in Germany could be written around the careers of the men who played a role in *Die Volkswohnung*. The emphasis would be on progress in a social rather than a formalistic or technological sense: human progress achieved through design, often of a deceptively rudimentary appearance. Among Walter Curt Behrendt's collaborators in this publishing venture were Otto Bartning, Walter Gropius, Erwin Gutkind, Gerhard Jobst, Ernst May, Paul Mebes, Leberecht Migge, Friedrich Paulsen, Paul Schmitthenner, Bruno Taut, and Martin Wagner; we shall encounter all of them in this study.

In spite of an economy which made it practically impossible to build anything, these idealistic men continued to devote themselves to the cause of providing decent housing for the working class. That their studies resulted initially in a great body of literature rather than in actual housing was no fault of their own. This material became the foundation for actual building in 1924 when the economy began to approach a state of normalcy once again.

### *Neues Bauen!:* Build Anew!

*Neues Bauen* was the watchword of architecture in Germany in the 1920s. It signifies not merely new building, but also has the electric quality of an urgent call to build new things, to start anew, to create a new architecture for a new society. The expression *Neues Bauen* appears again and again in titles for articles and books ranging from how-to practical handbooks concerning everything from financing to furnishing to guidebooks describing what had been achieved

In the latter category, one of the best known guidebooks is *Neues Bauen in Berlin,*[10] published in 1931, which serves as a convenient survey of what had been achieved in the period here under consideration. Setting the stage at the beginning of this period of housing revolution is another book with "new building" in its title, Erwin Gutkind's *Neues Bauen: Grundlagen zur praktischen Siedlungstätigkeit,* which was published in 1919 with the assistance of a group of housing specialists and the stated purpose of smoothing the way for the actual practice of building housing settlements.

In his foreword to Gutkind's book, Adolf Scheidt, the Reich's commissioner for housing and an undersecretary in the Prussian Ministry for Public Welfare, characterized the contemporary situation as follows:

> Build anew!—that is the cry today of all peoples after four years of terribly destructive battles. New building in all areas of man's thought and creativity is sorely needed after such protracted and thorough destruction. New building, furthered in the spirit of mutual help, can heal many wounds and cure much of the damage that this holocaust has brought.[11]

Scheidt went on to say that, in a practical sense, the rebuilding of the sorely disturbed spiritual and economic life of Germany could only begin with a concern for new housing. With a great sense of urgency he repeated the imperative, *Neues Bauen!*, that is, "Build anew!" However, he recognized and listed the problems standing in the way of an adequate building program: a severe shortage of building materials, a great lack of transportation,and an incredible rise in building costs. Scheidt made a revealing comment on the spirit of the times by concluding that the generally prevalent reluctance to undertake new projects or even to do any serious work at all in face of the highly unstable political situation was the greatest hindrance of all. He felt that it was imperative in the political upheaval of 1919 to prepare for a resumption of building activity.

The purpose, then, of Gutkind's book was to clarify the prevailing conditions and to provide practical guidelines for building low-density settlements in newly initiated workers' housing programs. In his initial chapter, also entitled *Neues Bauen,* Gutkind took up the theme of the seemingly insurmountable social and economic obstacles in 1919, while simultaneously insisting that something had to be done to stimulate new building activity. He demonstrated political awareness and sensitivity to current revolutionary conditions by commenting that questions of food and housing were the foundation stones upon which a stable political situation must be built. Despite the contrast between the many idealistic schemes on paper and the few that were realized, he felt these plans to be a great step forward since they showed so well the great need for a new approach to housing: low-rise, low-density settlements in contact with nature. Until 1914 there had been little recognition of any urgency for such a transformation, he commented, and no noticeable pressure to create single-family housing in low-rise buildings. The time now was ripe for bold men to overcome difficulties and to seize the initiative in beginning a new era.

Among the experts who participated in this fundamental handbook with Gutkind were Walter Curt Behrendt, Otto Bartning, Gerhard Jobst, and the landscape architect Leberecht Migge. Friedrich Paulsen, editor of *Die Bauwelt* and a specialist on standardization and rationalization in building, was also one of them. Yet among all those who contributed so much in this difficult time to developing concepts for advanced social housing in Germany, however, one man stands out as a major moving force in guiding developments in Berlin toward achievement of housing reform. This man, who was later to become the building commissioner of Greater Berlin, was Martin Wagner.

Wagner typified the progressive social idealism of the majority socialists, i.e., the Social Democratic Party (SDP), which administered Prussia and major cities during the Weimar Republic. Although this idealism was ultimately to collapse under the violent repression of the Nazis, it represents one of the most admirable qualities of the Weimar Republic. Without much danger of exaggeration it can be stated that the majority of the active reformers mentioned here were enthusiastic Social Democrats. It was to Martin Wagner's lasting credit that he was able to guide the diverse and often conflicting forces of architecture, planning, finance, construction, labor unions, and municipal bureaucracies toward the building of low-cost housing according to enlightened principles.

In 1919, however, the situation looked extremely grim. Everywhere there were great difficulties. The first step was to recognize and define the problems; the second was to present concrete proposals for overcoming them. In order to solve the problems of lack of land, money, manpower, and materials, it was necessary to resort to drastic and imaginative methods. The political revolution had passed without an accompanying revolution in land distribution. The social revolution, however, made it a matter of government policy to grant appropriate agencies necessary authority and funds to initiate a meaningful reform of housing. The solution of the housing crisis was above all else a political task, and the degree of reform accomplished was truly revolutionary.

# 3

# Building Code and Building Corporations

## Introduction

Housing in Berlin and its suburbs prior to the First World War had been in the grip of an old tradition. A building which did not utilize the maximum allowable space down to the last cubic meter was an anomaly; builders thought themselves cheated if the site had not been fully exploited, if the maximum rentable volume had not been enclosed. The overly permissive building code consisted merely of a patchwork of preventative measures designed basically to limit the degree of abuse.[1]

Because of this, an important device for carrying out the politics of housing reform was legislation to establish new building codes, not just with the negative goal of limiting bad practices, but with the positive goal of encouraging desirable forms of housing. A new building code had the potential of transforming the entire character of urban housing for the working class. By applying lessons from housing research, the code could bring about the building of appealing, healthful, low-density settlements. By contrast, old codes, such as that of Berlin, had had the effect of transforming barely tolerable housing into the norm. Of course, attempts had been made earlier to raise that norm. Pioneering studies of city planning advocated loosening up the urban fabric well before the First World War. The best early formation of these progressive concepts as they applied to Berlin was published by the Association of Berlin Architects in 1907 as a series of guidelines for a competition to design a regional plan for the envisioned greater Berlin.[2] Yet the Berlin code was still predicated upon mass housing in multistory tenements. Since this type of construction dominated, all zoning provisions were concerned with it, and the result was that the building of small houses was effectively discouraged.[3]

Berlin became one of the most important centers for the development of modern city planning. Establishing a coherent system of open spaces and greenery was one of the basic principles, which first saw realization after the war. Significantly, Martin Wagner, who became building and planning commissioner *(Stadtbaurat)* of greater Berlin in 1926 and had great influence on the city's architecture and planning in the later twenties, wrote his dissertation at the *Technische Hochschule* in Charlottenburg on open spaces in the metropolis in 1915.[4]

## Formation of Greater Berlin

Berlin did not become Greater Berlin until Charlottenburg and other adjacent cities, towns, plantations, and other smaller jurisdictions were incorporated in 1920. A total of ninety-three separate entities were unfied by this merger, making Berlin Europe's largest city in terms of area.[5] The creation of this vast entity enabled a unified city planning scheme to be effected for an entire urban region, a major step forward. By establishing a centralized authority, the legal means were provided by which the urban fabric could be loosened, one of the most striking features of the *Seidlungen* of the late twenties.

Yet strict zoning was not the only device employed by Berlin and other German cities in reducing density of development and establishing a network of public open spaces. Direct government purchase of enormous tracts of land gave the best assurance that land would be used to the best advantage of all. A crucial fact, rarely considered in recent literature on housing, is that approximately eighty percent of the land used by cooperative building societies and public benefit building corporations to build workers' settlements was owned by the city.

Under normal economic and political circumstances it would have been virtually impossible to make a sudden shift in emphasis to low-density settlements. Pressures from building speculators would have prevented it. Only the abnormally low price of land in relationship to the high building costs in the post-war period made such a shift politically feasible. An unfavorable economic situation in a political atmosphere favorable to socialization was turned to great advantage by the municipalities. They bought up large tracts of land in and around cities, creating vast forest preserves which remain to the present day, and placed parcels of land at the disposal of the non-profit building organizations in programs which provided most of the progressive housing of the 1920s.

## The New Building Code

Transforming the building code was a crucial step for Berlin and all cities. On April 25, 1919, the Prussian state commission for housing and welfare published a building code that was intended to serve as a model for all Prussian cities. Among its important provisions was the encouragement of low-cost housing in low-density settlements. Although Berlin did not enact its official code as law until November 3, 1925, the Prussian model was followed in practice throughout the 1920s. The Housing Welfare Office *(Wohnungsfürsorgegesellschaft)* had control over the disbursement of public funds to finance housing construction and used this control to enforce the new provisions.

An essential aspect of the new code was the severe control it exercised over the utilization of land. All land that had been or could be used for housing was divided into five classes (fig. 3). Classes I and II were open construction allowing a maximum of two full stories and a maximum area coverage of, respectively, ten and twenty percent, and floor/area ratios of only two-tenths and four-tenths. The other three classes and four subclasses increased allowable heights, areas and floor/area ratios to maximums of five stories, sixty percent, and three in Class V. Only in the inner core of the city was Class V allowed. The most important aspect of this code was the sharp distinction drawn between built-up land and land yet to be developed.

All new land that could be used for housing development in Greater Berlin was automatically placed under Class I of the new building code. This required that new housing on such land would be low-density, i.e., two-story buildings with a minimum of 500 square meters of site for each dwelling unit. No more than ten percent of the site could be covered by buildings in this class. Other provisions of the new code served further to humanize housing conditions by forbidding basement apartments and independent attic apartments, requiring adequate cross-ventilation, and requiring that each apartment have at least one principal room open to sunshine.

Among the provisions designed to eliminate dark, damp and otherwise unsuitable spaces from consideration as habitations were also rules to prohibit back and side buildings within blocks. The dismal air shafts and so-called *Berliner-Zimmer* (i.e., interior-corner rooms lighted by a window at one corner only), which were found at the inside angle of the "L" in normal tenement houses, were consigned to the past.[7] Minimal floor/area ratios and the necessity of leaving ninety percent of new land unbuilt guaranteed low density and assured low-rise buildings. These could be detached or semi-detached, but were usually row houses, generally arranged around the perimeter of blocks, with the entire center kept open for gardens. This was the pure peripheral form *(reine Randbebauung)*.

## Small Houses in Garden Settlements

Relative to the planning of interior and exterior spaces, style was a minor factor in these housing projects. Esthetically, the primary aim was a sense of unity, which could be achieved in different ways: by joining units into a

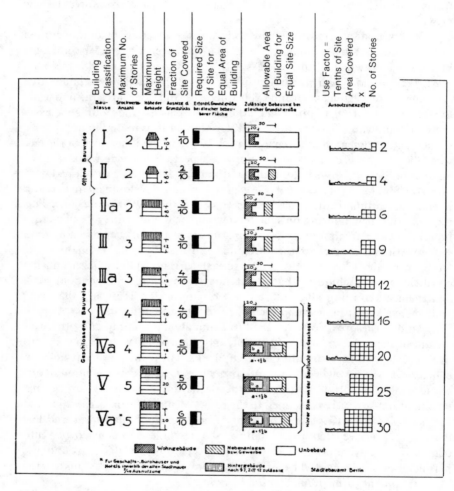

Figure 3.  Berlin building classification according to the Building Code of 1925, based on the Model Code for Prussia of 1919

(Gut, *Der Wohnungsneubau in Deutschland,* p. 95)

continuous perimeter around a large garden space, by linking smaller numbers of units together to form a discontinuous chain, by clustering buildings around spaces smaller than a whole block, or by surrounding lower buildings with taller ones, i.e., gradation. The visual relationship of parts to each other and to the whole could be achieved through the repetition of large and small architectural elements, or through the use of related or repeated colors, textures, materials, or masses. Small connecting elements, such as walls or utility buildings, could be used to draw larger parts together and heighten the effect of unity. Often, in larger settlements as we shall see, peripheral buildings would be one story taller, surrounding and seemingly protecting the row houses within. Entrances to complexes were often given a distinctive treatment as portals and nodal points and were usually combined with cooperative shops, meeting places, or other communal facilities.

From the end of the war until after 1925, "every housing reformer believed that the ideal home was a small house with attached garden; anything else could be nothing more than an unfortunate compromise due to uncontrollable circumstances."[8] This assertion by Catherine Bauer applies exactly to Bruno Taut's ideal city scheme, developed in 1919 as *The City Crown (Die Stadtkrone)*. Although the title of his book implies a preoccupation with monumental urban centers, Taut was thinking very much about the character of residential areas, writing that "their development is entirely in the character of the garden city, with low rows of houses and deep gardens for each house . . . so that the housing areas themselves are considered as a garden zone."[9]

The rhetorical question that had been asked by the ninth International Housing Congress in Vienna in 1910—*"Kleinhaus oder Mietskaserne?"*—was answered even more firmly in favor of the small house after the war. In Germany the difference between pre-war theory and post-war practice was essentially political. The abdication of the monarchy, the social ferment of the November Revolution, and a strong spirit of reform in the young republic created a climate favorable to change. Along with new laws and regulations concerning working hours and conditions, health and retirement insurance, the right to organize and the right to strike, provisions were also made to reform housing for the working class. Once it had been stated in the constitution that everyone had the right to a decent place to live, and once the decision had been made that the government should encourage and sponsor an effective program to attain that end, it remained to determine an appropriate mechanism to carry out the program. Cooperative building organizations, closely allied to the labor unions, were seen as the logical choice.

## Cooperative Building Organizations

Before the war, little had been accomplished in reforming workers' housing, although initial steps had been taken by the relatively small building cooperatives called *Baugenossenschaften*. Increasing numbers of such cooperatives—organized by the labor unions and other consumer self-help groups—had sprung up in the late nineteenth and early twentieth centuries, yet their contribution to the overall housing volume was minor, amounting to less than one percent of total housing construction in Berlin in 1910. For the most part, they were small self-help groups of individuals searching for adequate housing, who were willing to pool their resources and invest some of their own labor in construction.

In Germany the history of cooperative building organizations goes back to November of 1847—just prior to the failed revolution and the appearance of Marx's *Communist Manifesto*—and the founding of the *Berliner gemeinnützigen Baugesellschaft*. This first organization of its type was founded by Victor Aimé Huber (1800–69), and was not communist but conservative and enjoyed the sponsorship of the then Crown Prince, who later became Kaiser Wilhelm I.[10] Yet this modest movement in the direction of paternalistic reform did not gain momentum at the time. Subsequent building organizations formed in the spirit of self-help came into existence in the years 1864–65, but growth really began following national unification in 1871. From a beginning in that year of just 17 such organizations, the number grew to 30 in 1872 and 50 in 1873. The number of *Baugenossenschaften* steadily increased from then on and reached a peak in 1914, when the total reached 1400.

During the war, all housing construction came to a virtual halt. Since only government subsidies could set it into motion again, control could be exerted to transform housing into a special branch of the economy, operated according to the greatest good for the greatest number. The concept was to support only public benefit building activity *(gemeinnützige Bautätigkeit)*, which came to predominate throughout the 1920s.

The *gemeinnützige Baugesellschaften* were pioneers in methods of organization and reform of land utilization. In their fight against oppressive living conditions, the *Baugenossenschaften* had achieved one of the most important rights of tenants: the inalienable right to the use of a dwelling. It became impossible for members of such organizations ever to be turned out of their dwellings. Furthermore, the principle of cooperative self-help enabled workers to pool their resources and undertake building activities beyond the capability of any individual among them. The organizations played a most significant role in reforming housing in Germany, especially in establishing new types and standards for low-cost dwellings.

## Public Benefit Building Cooperations

The first of the major labor union-sponsored limited dividend building organizations was conceived in 1917 and founded as a corporation on August 14, 1918, as GAGFAH *(Gemeinnützige Aktiengesellschaft für Angestellten Heimstätten)*, i.e., public benefit corporation for salaried employees' homesteads. Two men, Hans Bechly, later chairman of the board of directors of GAGFAH, and Hermann Frank, later a member of the board, were instrumental in setting up this organization. Bechly had written an informational booklet concerning housing for salaried employees, entitled *Die Heimstätte des Angestellten,* which was influential in bringing various unions together. It presented a concrete proposal and stimulated the unified action of these labor organizations. Before the war was over they had their charter as a limited dividend corporation in the public interest and also had assured financing from the national insurance organization for these employees, *Die Reichsversicherungsanstalt für Angestellte.*[11]

The initial aim of GAGFAH was to free workers from the cramped and unhygienic conditions of the rental barracks, but other important considerations were the opportunity for salaried employees both to buy their own homes and still to be able to change positions and move to other cities. GAGFAH therefore was intended from the beginning to be a national rather than a local organization. Within the first ten years of its existence the corporation was able to erect a total of 16,000 units in different parts of Germany, and over two-thirds of these dwellings were either one or two-story row houses with gardens.

In 1922 the blue collar General Federation of German Unions (*Allgemeiner Deutscher Gewerkschaftsbund* or ADGB) addressed itself to housing problems at its congress in Leipzig. At the same time congresses of the other unions representing white collar workers (*Allgemeiner freier Angestelltenbund* or AFA) and civil servants (*Allgemeiner Deutscher Beamtenbund* or ADB) also turned their attention to this pressing problem and decided that they had to take an active role economically by purchasing construction materials in quantity and organizing largescale construction projects. Thus the financial power of organized labor was applied to finding a solution for the acute housing crisis.[12]

The ADGB organized its housing development cooperative in 1924 under the name of the German Housing Welfare Corporation for Civil Servants, Salaried Employees, and Workers (*Deutsche Wohnungsfürsorge Aktiengesellschaft für Beamte, Angestellte und Arbeiter* or DEWOG). The specific purpose of DEWOG was to act as an intermediary between the working classes and the government, that is, to promote and expand the principle and practice of a truly non-profit, cooperative economic system in housing construction, so that the broad spectrum of the populace could benefit. In practice, DEWOG took over the technical and financial administration of building projects for many small building organizations; it also formed its own subsidiaries. Thus, in Berlin, one of the most interesting organizations of the 1920s was formed as the capital's operating subsidiary of DEWOG. It was called GEHAG, an acronym for *Gemeinnützige Heimstätten-, Spar- und Bau-Aktiengesellschaft*, i.e., Public Benefit Homestead, Savings, and Building Corporation, although, in fact, it did not exercise the option of functioning as a savings bank. [13]

GEHAG was organized to build in Berlin, although it later expanded its activities to other parts of Germany. Along with DEWOG, its shareholders included blue-collar workers' unions, an association of banks, the socialized building trades, and various *Baugenossenschaften* with such utopian names as *Freie Scholle* (free soil), *Ideal*, and *Paradies*. From the beginning GEHAG was closely associated with the labor movement and overtly socialistic in its goals. As we shall see, these associations allied GEHAG with the policies of the Social Democratic administrations of Berlin and of Prussia and led to overt esthetic expression of its socialistic leanings. Martin Wagner, who was to become building commissioner of Berlin, was on the board of directors of GEHAG from the beginning, and Bruno Taut became its chief architect. In the eight-year period from 1924 to 1932 GEHAG erected a total of 9,300 housing units in Berlin. A building program of such magnitude was bound to have a major impact on Berlin's urban development, and specific efforts were made to develop new, exemplary solutions for the planning of housing in large cities.

The entire Berlin housing program was based on the social principles of helping those most in need of help, i.e., the low-income working population. Joint statements emphasizing the pressing need for low-cost, high-quality housing for the masses and calling for a large construction program were made by the three socialist union federations, the ADGB, AFA and ADB. In November of 1926 they again presented a thorough description of needs and justification of their position. This was published as *Guidelines for Housing Construction (Richtlinien für den Wohnungsbau)* and called for a national building program to provide a quarter of a million *Volkswohnungen* annually. Although the more conservative Christian labor unions were also active in building housing for government workers, white collar and blue collar workers—since the housing shortage hit every segment of society—they were less active in the politics of housing and had considerably less impact in terms of quantity built.

The greatest pressure to reform workers' housing came from the majority socialist (SPD) camp, with the independent or radical socialists and the communists essentially disinclined to participate, since they spurned any reform as accommodation to a corrupt bourgeois system. The communist view was that oppressive living conditions would serve to hasten the inevitable demise of capitalism, and hence relieving the crisis could only be counterproductive. Therefore, the architects who made the major contributions to the reform of workers' housing in the Weimar Republic tended to be in the socialist camp.

One demonstration of the intimate relationship between the public service building corporations, the unions, and the Social Democratic Party is the name of Bruno Taut's *Gross-Siedlung* in Prenzlauer Berg, *Carl Legien Stadt* (to be discussed in chapter 7). Carl Legien, born in 1861, had been a major figure in national and international labor unions. He served for many years as an SPD deputy to the *Reichstag;* was head of the ADGB labor federation; from 1903 to 1919 headed the International Association of Labor Unions *(Internationale Vereinigung der Gewerkschaften);* and, shortly before his death in 1920, served as president of the National Economic Council where—in calling for the general strike of the unions—he helped bring about the failure of the Kapp Putsch. GEHAG, in naming its settlement after Legien and prominently displaying his name in large letters on one of the buildings, clearly expressed not only its admiration for the man but its solidarity with the ideas he represented. Socialism and the striving for a better life for the working class were thus clearly and overtly supported by GEHAG.

Although the unification of Berlin building cooperatives *(Baugenossenschaften)* with the building corporations *(Baugesellschaften)* was only partial, the joining of forces among building associations, building trades, and trade unions was achieved; and GEHAG was the result. In Berlin this public service building corporation was the means by which the large scale, exemplary building of homes for the working class could be carried out. Its founding was a milestone on the road to achieving the idealistic goals for housing reform set by its predecessors and contemporaries in the labor movement. In the *GEHAG-Festschrift* Martin Wagner was given credit for key ideas and leadership in the founding of this organization, which played such an important role in Berlin.[14] Its activities were aimed at improving public welfare generally, and specifically making decent housing available to the broad masses of skilled and unskilled workers.

GEHAG thus strove to provide comfortable apartments which could be rented cheaply and inexpensive row houses which could be purchased with long-term, low-interest mortgages. To prevent speculation and the raising of prices, GEHAG and all other true public benefit corporations required that the houses could only be resold to the organization itself at no profit. This provision not only kept prices down but assured long-term continuity of residents, which had—and still has—very salutary effects on the spirit of solidarity in these settlements. Many of the residents today are sons and daughters of the original residents.

The benevolent role of socialism in the reform of Berlin housing in the 1920s seems well epitomized by the person of Martin Wagner. Besides writing a dissertation on public green spaces in cities and coming up with the idea of the house-rent tax as a means of financing a public housing program, he was a leading figure in the national movement to socialize the building trades—serving as chairman of the board of the *Berliner Bauhütte*—and was a founding director of GEHAG as well as its chief of planning. He was the building councilor for the borough of Schöneberg in the years immediately after the war; and, when Wagner was chosen as the building councilor or commissioner *(Stadtbaurat)* for Greater Berlin on October 28, 1926, the stage was set for major accomplishments in Berlin *Siedlungen*. As *Stadtbaurat,* Wagner saw his role as analogous to that of a contemporary film director, organizing, planning, directing, letting individual architects—such as Bruno Taut and Hans Scharoun—play the starring roles, yet providing overall guidance and leadership at all levels.

The interrelationship between architecture and socialism was made explicit in a 1926 article, whose author, Max Jahn, stressed the social function of architecture in providing shelter for the masses and improving living standards. He concluded that "although neither socialism nor architecture has achieved its final goal, a major victory has been won. Capital is serving the cause of socialism in that it is facilitating the most social function of architecture, i.e., creating small apartments and *Siedlungen*."[16] Looking at the accomplishments described in chapters 6 and 7, one would have to agree with this assessment; yet, it is one of the ironies of the era that the Social Democratic Party did not always live up to the ideals of its founders and leading figures. Early in 1931 there was a falling out between Martin Wagner and the SPD—ostensibly due to a trip Wagner had taken to Moscow—and Wagner withdrew from party membership. While the realization of socialistic principles is a basic theme of this study, we must realize that principles and party politics were not always in close harmony.

# 4

# The Practical Dwelling
# (Die Gebrauchswohnung)

Economy and practicality were the essentials demanded of workers' housing. To emphasize these attributes a special term was employed during the twenties: the practical dwelling *(die Gebrauchswohnung),* for which planning was far more important than esthetics. Since housing costs were calculated on a per square meter basis, every unnecessary square meter raised the price of a housing unit and made it that much less affordable to the working class. Since available public funds had to be used to build as many units as possible, minimum size was considered essential, efficient planning crucial. Yet, although economies of various kinds were instituted, little was done to rethink the layout of a low cost dwelling until fairly late in the decade.

Although simple, the standard plan employed throughout most of the decade in most projects financed with public funds did have many advantages. Healthful exposure to fresh air, direct sunshine and greenery was the first prerequisite, as we have seen; hence it was required that both row houses and apartment buildings be no more than two rooms deep, with all rooms facing outward, ideally toward gardens rather than streets. Assured through-ventilation was another great advantage over earlier dwelling forms.

For row houses, the standard developed was a three-and-one-half-room, three-story plan, one room wide. The principal room at ground level was the living room, with a bedroom in each of the stories above, as can be seen in the accompanying typical plan. On the other side of the house, because of the stairway and the bath, only a half-room was available. At ground level this was the kitchen, on the second story a child's bedroom, and at the top a storage space which could be converted into yet another child's bedroom. A modest widening of this plan enabled the placement of another half-room adjacent to the kitchen (with the stair moved to a location adjacent to the living room). This sufficed to transform the basic plan into the standard for a four-and-one-half-room house (with attic storage space convertible to an additional small bedroom). Fundamental to these designs was the concept that, while the rooms might be as small as possible, every separate living function was still to be carried out in a separate room, i.e., cooking in the kitchen, eating and sitting in the living room, sleeping in separate bedrooms. The main disadvantage was the constant climbing of stairs required of the housewife.

Plans for dwelling units in apartment houses followed the same principles, except that each unit was all on one level (fig. 4). This, too, was essentially a rowhouse arrangement, with each dwelling being a through-unit, only two rooms deep and having outside windows on both sides. The unit was required to be entered via an internal staircase, and each room had to be a separate entity. This dictated that all rooms, including kitchen and bath, had to open from a central entry space *(Diele* or *Flur),* which could vary in size and proportion, but which usually was quite small. The requirement of exposure on both sides of the building meant that only two apartments could open off each landing. While the building in theory could be indefinitely long, an entrance and stairway would have to be interposed after every two dwelling units. Thus, the "two-span type" *(Zweispännertyp)* became the standard for multiple-unit housing. The logical consequence was the development of "strip," "band," or "slab" housing, extensible in length and height, but strictly limited in depth or thickness. From the standpoint of exterior design, another consequence was the dissappearance of a distinction between the front and back in such buildings.

Perhaps because all of this was a vast improvement over pre-war standards, few people seem to have been aware that a fundamental reconsideration of the basic floor plan could lead to still more important changes in the practical dwelling. Neither Walter Gropius nor Bruno Taut nor any other famous architect in Germany devoted much attention to changing the standard plans before 1927 (although Mies van der Rohe developed a scheme for a flexible plan with movable partitions at the *Weissenhof Seidlung* in Stuttgart in that year). Yet many reformers of various professions were giving serious consideration to social, psychological, technological, and other aspects of the ordinary dwelling and to means of analyzing and improving it. From an architectural point of view, the best synthesis of research on dwelling plans was provided by one man, Alexander Klein.

Although Klein himself openly acknowledged his debt to the important work of other researchers, he was the first architect in Germany to publicize a thorough system for analyzing and designing plans for small dwelling units. He began to publish the results of his studies in 1927, and in 1928, at the International Congress for Housing and Planning in Paris, he presented his concepts to a wide audience of architects and planners, winning considerable acclaim for the practical value of his approach. Klein's system began with a division of the important factors to be considered into four categories: the general grouping of rooms; the sizes and proportions of rooms, their interconnections, and the location of doors; the orientation of the dwelling unit for exposure to sunshine; and the design and furnishing of the interior.[1]

Concerning the general grouping of rooms, Klein felt it important that the main rooms should not serve as corridors and that they should be clearly divided into two groups: bedrooms, bath and toilet on the one hand, and living room, kitchen and loggia on the other. This made it possible clearly to distinguish the various living functions of sleeping and washing, cooking and eating, working and resting, and to allow them to be carried out simultaneously without wasting steps and without interfering with each other. The sleeping group, Klein felt, should be separated from the living group by a neutral space in order to assure greater quiet. Especially important in Klein's plans were the close linkages of bathroom to bedrooms and of kitchen to dining room. Furthermore, a loggia or balcony was desirable to provide an opportunity to step into the fresh air (and to air the bedding, a cherished German custom).

Concerning sizes and relationships of rooms and locations of doors and windows, an important consideration in Klein's system was maximizing unbroken floor area with furniture in place. Optimal proportioning and arranging to obtain unified, open floor areas helped avoid a sense of constriction, especially in small dwellings. While the number of separate units of space in a dwelling could be kept to a minimum, Klein was opposed to the most common form of such economy: the so-called living-kitchen (*Wohnküche*), because, he felt, cooking tends to impinge too much on the other uses of a living room. Instead, the living room should be the hub of a family's activity; any differentiation of separate work spaces from the living room was to be done with drapes, or with folding or sliding doors—preferably of glass—in order to retain the greatest effect of spaciousness.

One aspect of Klein's planning common to many contemporaries was the stress that was placed on geographic orientation and consequent exposure to sunlight. They recognized then as we seem to be rediscovering today that sunlight not only is important for health and comfort, but also has favorable psychological effects. An east-west orientation of dwellings, therefore, was considered most desirable, but an orientation toward the south was also highly favored. In the preferred east-west arrangement, the bedrooms were to be on the east side of the house, to catch the morning sun, while the living room was to face west to receive the evening sun when the family was together after work.

Klein's idea concerning furnishings and interior design was to create light, open and unified spaces. Ease of living, freedom of movement and lack of clutter were the impressions he sought. The centers of rooms should be kept free, furniture should be arranged close to walls, and windows should be

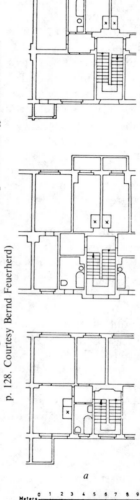

Figure 4. Berlin standard plans for apartments in the 1920s
*a*, one-and-one-half room plans; *b*, two room plans; *c*, two-and-one-half room plans.
(Schallenberger and Kraffert, *Berliner Wohnungsbauten aus öffentlichen Mitteln*, p. 128. Courtesy Bernd Feuerherd)

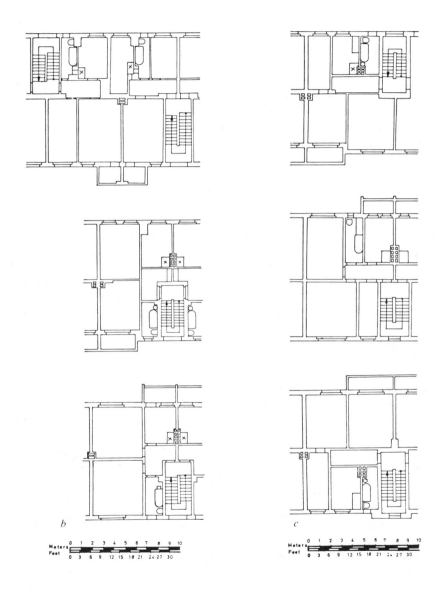

_b_                                               _c_

Meters   0 1 2 3 4 5 6 7 8 9 10
Feet     0 3 6 9 12 15 18 21 24 27 30

Meters   0 1 2 3 4 5 6 7 8 9 10
Feet     0 3 6 9 12 15 18 21 24 27 30

unified, allowing an unbroken sweep of light across the floor and a sense of uniform brightness throughout.

Before the articulation of Klein's system, concepts such as spatial form, spatial sequence, traffic paths, clarity, efficiency, etc., had become almost totally subjective, depending more on the eye of the beholder than on inherent characteristics of the architecture in question. After having his eyes opened by Klein, Werner Hegemann found most architects of the day, himself included, guilty of designing more for the sake of form than for the sake of effectiveness. Klein did so much to remove the veil from and clarify the basic issues of floor plans that Hegemann—in the pages of *Wasmuths Monatshefte,* over the subtitle "analysis of plans in the spirit of Alexander Klein"—asked the rhetorical question, "Schmitthenner, Bruno Taut Etc.: Slaves of a Misunderstood Classicism?"[2]

Hegemann reported that Klein's system had stimulated much grateful praise from architects at home and abroad, especially since he provided a graphic method for analyzing the traffic patterns and actual paths necessary for using a particular plan. This included a study of the directness and shortness of paths and the amount of floor area lost to traffic routes. The second factor measured was the degree of concentration of the paths and the spaciousness of the dwelling after the placement of necessary furniture. In this, the optical and psychological effects of shadows cast were taken into account. The third factor to be measured by graphic means was the geometrical similarity and logical relationship of the unified portions of floor area that should be perceived by an observer entering each room. Klein's studies showed that the psychological effects of a dwelling depend to a large extent upon the character and relationships of such unified surfaces.

Similar and closely related to the effects of area components on the floor were the effects of unified areas on vertical surfaces. The fourth factor to be measured in Klein's analysis was the degree of unity of wall surfaces and the measurable effects of spaciousness or confinement they created. As with the floors, calculable shadow patterns on the vertical surfaces were significant in analyzing the optical and psychological effects of a dwelling.

Only natural light and general furniture shapes were considered in these calculations. Klein recognized that artificial light and particular furnishings could do much to enhance or diminish the inherent values of any dwelling unit, but this systematic approach was intended to encourage designs which aimed for the highest possible inherent spatial value without artificial aids. Creating a high quality of life in even the most economical of small apartments was the most significant potential benefit of Klein's system.

It is this striving for fundamental human benefits through design that characterized what can be called the socialization of architecture in Berlin in the 1920s. A social rather than stylistic approach to architectural design is what made this work so significant and what makes it still relevant today. Although Alexander Klein's system did not become the standard in Berlin, the spirit and method of his approach to the problem seem particularly representative of the period. One may recognize in Klein the image of the technocrat at work serving community interests. Unfortunately for him, his emphasis on social values rather than on a striking personal style deprived Klein of general recognition in the history of modern architecture. In the context of the present study, however, his approach is of great interest.

Klein used the comparative method in his 1928 publication (fig. 5). Two moderate-sized apartments of equal floor area were chosen. One, considered a typical plan of the time although not identified as such, was actually from the *Siedlung Ceciliengärten,* discussed in chapter 6; the other was an improved design, in keeping with Klein's principles. The disadvantages of the traditional plan were given as follows: no uniform orientation of the rooms; no grouping of rooms; inconvenient relationship between the cooking-eating and the sleeping-washing spaces; no freedom of movement, due to the unfavorable arrangement of furniture; the shading of one of the bedrooms behind the loggia; unfavorable lighting of the rooms by two or three openings along a relatively short front; no quiet area for sitting or working; and a large entryway with six doors, useless for anything but traffic.

By contrast, Klein presented his alternative as striving toward order and spaciousness and having the following characteristics: clear separation of the rooms into two main groups, the living-eating group directly connected to the loggia and the sleeping group directly connected to the bath and toilet; the joining of the living and the eating space with the possibility of separation by a drape or folding door; kitchen reduced in size in favor of the living room; clothing storage in a separate closet room acting as a sound buffer and lighted by a glass door to the bath; favorable relationship of loggia to both kitchen and dining area and the latter two connected by a pass-through; beds located in the darker parts of the bedrooms with the lightest areas reserved for free movement; and concentrated location of furniture and use of built-in closets and storage shelves to achieve larger, unified floor and wall surfaces.

Klein's system as here outlined provided the means to greatly improve the living value of modest dwellings. His approach was clearly understandable, simple, and direct. Its oft repeated publication and the acclaim he received for it might lead one to expect a basic change in the plans of workers' housing. Such a change, however, did not come about. Neither GEHAG nor GAGFAH nor any other major public service building corporation changed its set of standard plans to conform with Klein's concepts, although Klein was commissioned to do some projects in accordance with his system. The standard plans described at the beginning of this chapter were unsophisticated and remained essentially unchanged through most of the decade. Even in

Figure 5. Comparison of traditional plan with Klein's improved design, Alexander Klein, with graphic analysis
Traditional plan on the left, Klein's on the right; *a*, layouts of rooms and furniture; *b*, analysis of paths for domestic functions; *c*, principal floor areas devoted to traffic; *d*, open and contiguous floor areas; *e*, distribution of shaded floor areas.

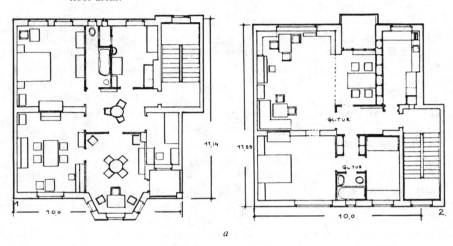

*a*

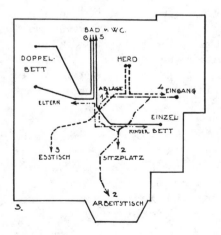

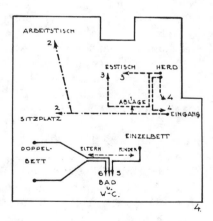

*b*

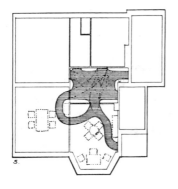

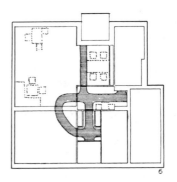

c

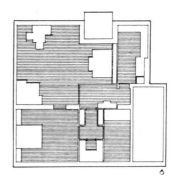

d

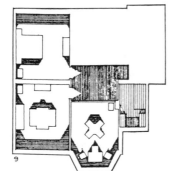

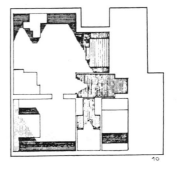

e

major *Siedlungen* the plans of the dwelling units were most often established by the building corporations, which left the planning of spaces, masses and appearances from the exterior as the primary concerns of architects. Therefore the latter aspects of the housing projects will be emphasized in the following presentations of representative projects.

The floor plans of dwelling units underwent a significant transformation in 1929, as did other major aspects of mass housing. Since it became apparent that the housing shortage was not being eliminated and that more stringent economies would have to be instituted, the number of rooms and the amount of dwelling area calculated per person were decreassed. In these very small units the specific arrangements envisioned by Alexander Klein were not incorporated; yet, since his devices for maximizing a sense of spaciousness were so well known from the literature, they contributed significantly to the development of acceptable small dwelling plans with a sense of openness. At the end of the decade, the design of a dwelling for "minimum existence" *(die Wohnung für das Existenzminimum)* was derived from the prior concepts of *Volkswohnung* and *Gebrauchswohnung.*

# 5

# The Dwelling for "Minimum Existence"

*Die Wohnung für das Existenzminimum* was perhaps a misnomer. The intention was not to keep people living at a subsistence level. It was intended to provide a healthful and pleasant living environment for those who earned only a subsistence wage. More public relations-conscious developers of subsequent decades came to call this product of the architectural and social research of the 1920s the "efficiency apartment." Yet "efficiency apartment" suggests only one limited aspect of the idea and implies neither the architects' new social consciousness nor their awareness of responsibility to low-income workers. *Existenzminimum* is a far more graphic concept that draws into focus the fact that large segments of the working class needed to be raised to the threshold of a decent way of life, to an acceptable dwelling in keeping with modern standards. Perhaps most interesting is the realization that architects were turning their attention away from architecture as a fine art and considering instead a stratum of the manmade environment usually beyond their purview: dwellings for the poor. Furthermore, they were actually creating something appealing rather than apalling. For these reasons, *die Wohnung für das Existenzminimum* is an appropriate name for a fundamental contribution of the 1920s to the development of modern architecture.

The design of good, small, highly efficient dwelling units for low-income families was the essential problem of progressive architects in Berlin and other German and European cities in the later years of the 1920s. Delegates to the first preliminary meeting in Basel to discuss formation of the C.I.A.M. *(Congrès Internationaux d'Architecture Moderne)* on February 2, 1928, decided that the theme of the 1929 Second International Congress of Modern Architecture would be the minimal dwelling. Furthermore, the Congress of the International Federation for Housing and Planning, held in Paris in 1928 (at which Klein made his presentation, mentioned earlier), also devoted its attention to the theme of dwellings for the poor.

Principal efforts in this direction—both within and without the C.I.A.M.—were popularized in a travelling exhibition sponsored by the

Frankfurt municipal building commission under the direction of Ernst May. This commission hosted the 1929 C.I.A.M. congress and co-sponsored the published summary of its findings, which appeared as *Die Wohnung für das Existenzminimum* in 1930.[1] This book, compiled by Siegfried Giedion, was very important, not only because it included many plans from the various proposals, but for its summary of the progressive attitudes toward the problem held by influential spokesmen of the time, including Walter Gropius, Ernst May, Siegfried Giedion, and Le Corbusier with Pierre Jeanneret.

Giedion set the tone of the C.I.A.M. investigation of the problem with his statement that architecture was the last major field of production to take the step to industrialization. He said that the standard three or four-story building was the result of traditional, non-industrial methods of construction. The potential inherent in the structural skeleton system which made it possible for dwellings to rise to many stories was important to him. High-rise buildings, he felt, allowed a greater possibility of satisfying "the new biological requirements" of man. By this he meant that tall buildings could be arranged to provide maximum space between them (presumably for parks and sports facilities). Furthermore, with a skeletal construction, dwelling plans could be free, flexible, and adaptable to new living requirements, and windows could be arranged to provide great amounts of daylight and fresh air. Yet at that time building ordinances everywhere in Europe prevented the construction of high-rise buildings for housing, and, in retrospect, one might conclude that they did so with good reason.

The emphasis on technology and the high-rise building is a familiar part of the polemics of the C.I.A.M. and the Bauhaus. Yet precisely this emphasis serves to separate theory from practice in the twenties. Contemporary housing construction, for the most part, employed neither sophisticated technology nor the high-rise building type. Giedion, who was executive secretary of C.I.A.M., stressed the group's theoretical stand, which had been articulated in 1928 at the first C.I.A.M. congress at La Sarraz, Switzerland. This was their programmatic rejection of the formal principles of earlier epochs. The men of C.I.A.M. sought to create an architecture appropriate to their time by devoting special attention to new building materials, new structural systems, and new production methods. However, this emphasis was reflected in Berlin only to a limited extent, primarily in experiments by Hans and Wassili Luckhardt and by Mebes and Emmerich, who adapted the steel frame to housing construction, and by the more frequent use of reinforced concrete. In Frankfurt Ernst May's development of concrete building components for housing drew wide attention, and the houses at Stuttgart-Weissenhof in 1927 had also emphasized the application of new materials and systems. Structural innovations, however, were not a major aspect of the Berlin *Siedlungen* of the 1920s.

Providing simple, healthful, and economical housing, on the other hand, was a major contribution. The goal of providing such housing for the poorest segment of society remained unattained in all lands—as indeed it remains today. The dire situation in Germany was graphically presented by the German Association for Housing Reform in its publication *Wohnungsnot und Wohnungselend in Deutschland,* which conservatively estimated that over one million families in Germany had no independent dwelling at all, irrespective of quality. It was part of the goal of C.I.A.M. and of all housing reformers to draw popular attention to such facts, to search for the underlying causes of the housing crisis, and to promote research into possible solutions to relieve both the housing shortage and oppressive housing conditions.

In Germany legislation of June 2, 1927 had established a Federal Society for Research in Building and Housing Economy (*Reichsforschungsgesellschaft für Wirtschaftlichkeit im Bau- und Wohnungswesen,* RFG for short) to carry out precisely this type of research into the economical, technical, and social problems related to housing. Among the architects mentioned in this study, several were on the administrative or research boards of the RFG from its inception, including Bruno Ahrends, Otto Bartning, Walter Gropius, Ernst May, Friedrich Paulsen, Paul Schmitthenner, and Eduard Jobst Siedler.[2] A fundamental problem, recognized by both the C.I.A.M. and the RFG, was to determine the type of dwelling appropriate for workers earning only a subsistence wage. But all aspects of housing were researched with great thoroughness by delegations, committees, and individual members of the RFG. Studies of planning included site planning and apartment planning, as well as planning of efficient furnishings and equipment for dwelling units. Building construction, too, was thoroughly analyzed, including materials, prefabrication, standardization, materials handling, etc. Experts from all branches of architecture and the construction industry pooled their knowledge and expertise with that of researchers in hygiene and sociology. Closely related to considerations of economy and efficiency were studies of minimum dwelling requirements based on biological and psychological needs of every person, no matter what his wage. Minimum needs had to be determined, minimum standards established. "Every man his due ration of dwelling" was the goal.

The oft-repeated question, "Do we need minimal dwellings?" when restated by Ernst May, became purely rhetorical. He considered minimal dwellings to be the best solution. Counterarguments, however, included the increased cost per square meter in smaller dwellings and the possibility of the negative psychological effects of overly small apartments. One alternative to minimal dwellings was a proposal that new housing units be built larger for those who could afford them while other dwellings be turned over to the poor, a predecessor to today's "trickle down" theories. Martin Wagner was among those who felt that arguments against building overly small units had merit, but Ernst May considered them unconvincing. May and Gropius were advocates of a technological approach. "Create dwellings that are healthy and livable—even if small—but, above all, provide them at bearable rents." This was the goal as May summarized it.[3] Basic to the approach of both the C.I.A.M. and the RFG was the assumption that research, systematic analysis, and technical progress would provide the best means to achieving the goal. The minimal dwelling was the product of their work. It would appear that the methodology of pseudo-scientific analysis and design of an efficient "machine for living" became an important end in itself. Emphasis upon handicraft, as in the early Bauhaus, was transformed into an emphasis upon the modern "craft" of technology. The attempt to cloak one's own work in an aura of science and technology was particularly evident in the writings of Walter Gropius. His essay for the International Congress concerning *Die Wohnung für das Existenzminimum* purported to treat "The Sociological Foundations for Minimal Dwellings for the Urban Populace."[4] In his essay, rather than presenting sociological foundations, Gropius quite correctly and quite simply identified socialization and the contemporary tendency toward smaller families as justification for smaller dwelling units. The socialization of labor, he said, had led to the socialization of a large portion of the functions of families; and this had led to an increasing independence of family members— including mothers—from each other. The family as a large production-consumption entity, in his view, had lost its significance. In its place had come more and more independent households of smaller size, which meant that the minimal dwelling was the answer to a genuine need and should not be considered as a temporary compromise. On the contrary, Gropius considered any encouragement of large apartments to be a false policy, which would only lead to multiple occupancies and subletting. He stressed the need to consider the positive aspects of minimal dwellings and carefully to study their planning rather than simply to reduce the size and number of rooms.

The principal requirements of minimal dwellings were the light, air, and space needed to develop life functions fully and without hindrance, according to Gropius. He felt that light and air were more essential than space. Therefore the solution was to be sought in enlarging windows and economizing on space. Yet every grown person was to be provided with his/her own room, be it ever so small. An anonymous Bauhaus photomontage of a man doubled up in a cubicle, labeled *"das Existenzminimum"* made the point by way of exaggeration. No matter how dire the contemporary situation, it was felt that every effort should be made to design a sensible, objective standard minimum. This could be designed for elemental functioning in a way analogous to a seat in an express train or a cabin in an ocean liner.

Gropius considered it a fundamental responsibility of society to provide "a due ration of dwelling" to everyone who worked. What was to be done for those who did not work was apparently not considered. The liberation of women was also a topical concern, and Gropius used the theme of the increasing spiritual and economic freedom of women as a major justification for the planning of communal facilities for certain basic household functions. The goal was to reduce the amount of domestic drudgery; it also justified further reducing the size of individual units.

Unfortunately, as Gropius reported, it had been the experience of all civilized countries during the twenties that it was impossible to satisfy the living needs of the masses in the face of the continuing discrepancy between wages and building costs, and especially in the face of continuing high rates of interest. Since technology was always subservient to industry and the commercial world, reductions in cost achieved through technological advances were primarily based on profits to investors. Here Gropius touched upon an important fact of the building industry. Perhaps without realizing it, he also provided a reason for the relatively slight impact of technological innovation on the construction of workers' housing in the twenties. Simplification and standardization played a major role; technical refinements, however, were less important in practice.

Among those who emphasized the need for rationalization and standardization as an essential step in achieving the highest degree of economy was Bruno Taut.[5] Of course, ever since 1920, rationalization and standardization had been matters of public policy advocated by the Welfare Ministry and the Ministry of Labor. Implementation was another matter. Taut recognized that the final stage in developing economical housing for the masses would be the prefabrication of major house components, which could be erected on a site regardless of the weather. Transformation of the building industry to a steady producer of building components under factory conditions would have been a significant advance in technology. Taut came out in favor of this change, which would have contributed to an economical housing-welfare program on a scale far greater than that achieved in Berlin. Such a change also would have transformed construction work from seasonal employment into a steady occupation. Martin Wagner felt that assembly line production and strong central control of the building process would have been "far more productive than thirty-six committee meetings of the *Reichsforschungsgesellschaft* and more productive than all of the brainstorms of architects striving to save a few marks on the plan of a small dwelling."[6]

Wagner's and Taut's practical attitudes led them to recognize that true economy could not be achieved via technological improvement alone. Even a thirty percent reduction in building costs, Taut said, might have little effect on reducing rents if the method of financing were not changed.[7] The ultimate barrier to achieving low-cost yet high-quality housing for the lowest income levels of society was the interest rate on mortgages. This view was echoed by Jakob Schallenberger of the Housing Welfare Office when he said, "The key to the rent problem lies in lowering the rate of interest on first mortgages."[8] This averaged about ten percent in Germany under normal conditions in the twenties. The economic situation in the Weimar Republic precluded seeking a solution to the problem of decent housing for the poor in government rent subsidies for existing buildings. Not enough buildings were available in the first place. Furthermore, capital on the open market was so scarce as to make it impossible to expect private industry to supply the housing needed to meet the demand, even if the government had been able to subsidize rents. Before the war first mortgages amounting to sixty to eight-five percent of total value had been available at a mere four percent interest. During the twenties first mortgages cost nine or ten percent and could only be had for forty percent of total value of the property. Second mortgages were extremely difficult to obtain on the open market and cost from twelve to fourteen percent. The most direct and most effective means of supporting workers' housing was thus seen to be the provision of second mortgages at low interest rates. One source of these funds was the House Rent Tax levied on pre-war buildings; another important source was the national insurance agencies, which provided funds to help build housing for insured workers.

In a 1931 report entitled *The Social Importance of Housing Now and in the Future,* it was conservatively calculated that support from public sources enabled financing costs to be reduced by almost half.[9] The example used to demonstrate this was a typical small dwelling costing nine thousand *Reichsmark* (RM):

The financing of a small dwelling, the total building costs of which amount to 9,000 RM, is approximately as follows:

| | |
|---|---|
| A first mortgage of 3,600 RM at 9% | 324.00 RM |
| Rent-Tax mortgage of 4,000 RM at 1% | 40.00 RM |
| General expenses | 90.00 RM |
| Total        = | 454.00 RM |

Without any support from public funds the financing would be as follows (assuming, of course, that the necessary capital was to be had at all):

| | |
|---|---|
| A first mortgage of 3,600 RM at 9% | 324.00 RM |
| A second mortgage of 4,000 RM at 10% | 400.00 RM |
| General expenses | 90.00 RM |
| Total        = | 814.00 RM |

The equity an owner had to supply to purchase a small dwelling generally was between ten and fifteen percent. The income of a person who would be considered able to buy such a dwelling with government financing was approximately 3500 marks per year. Unfortunately, this was considerably above the general working-class average in Germany during normal times in the twenties. The program of making cheap building money available for the construction of workers' housing was not tied to the low level of income of the prospective occupants. The program was a general economic device geared to current conditions rather than a device for assisting particularly needy families. The intent was to place the ownership or rental of new housing units within the reach of a large segment of the wage-earning populace, but it did not always work as intended.

In addition to the direct method of providing building capital from public sources at low interest rates, the government also supported housing construction by indirect devices. Tax relief was perhaps the most important of these and was used particularly to encourage the activities of public benefit building corporations and building cooperatives. Such organizations essentially were relieved of taxes, thus enabling them to further reduce the costs of the units they built. When it became evident that many builders were utilizing these tax breaks for private gain rather than public welfare, it became necessary to tighten the qualifications for a building organization wishing to be designated as *gemeinnützig,* i.e., in the public interest.

But let us return to the people whose housing needs were so desperate and for whom the new housing was intended. A comparison of income to cost of living and cost of housing serves to clarify the difficulty of trying to provide good, new housing for the masses. It was calculated that the average annual income of skilled workers was 2,784 RM, or 54.12 RM per week; for unskilled workers the annual average was 2,148 RM, or 41.80 RM per week. But the average cost of living—without housing—for a family of four (one child no older than ten, a second child no older than five) was 44.00 RM per week. This figure, calculated for a physiologically acceptable minimum—29.00 RM for food, 2.20 RM for heat and light, 5.60 RM for clothing, and 7.20 RM for taxes, insurance and miscellaneous—already exceeded the average wage of a fully employed unskilled worker and did not include anything for housing.

How did they manage? The answer lies in another statistic: the average worker was able to meet only eighty percent of the basic cost of living from his wages. The remaining twenty percent had to be supplied by a second job, the wife's working, contributions or work of the children, subletting a part of the apartment or the use of a bed, or from some other source.

Under such economic conditions it was calculated that a bearable weekly rent could seldom be as high as ten marks, and that even this figure could be considered only if there were some assurance that the tenant would remain regularly employed and that he would receive the standard wage. Fifty-two percent of the wage-earning populace could afford to pay less than five marks per week for housing. The melancholy conclusion of the calculation of bearable rents was that, under the then current conditions, there would be many families for whom even the lowest rents would still be too high.[10]

It remains to consider the actual costs and the rents charged for the new housing developments of the twenties. In 1930 a survey conducted by the International Association for Housing showed that in Berlin the net building costs of an apartment (with stove heating) of 56.84 square meters usable area were as follows: In a two-story house the cost was 33.00 RM per cubic meter of enclosed space and 171.60 RM per square meter of usable area; in a three-story building a similar dwelling cost 32.75 RM per cubic meter and 153.93 per square meter; while in a four-story building such a dwelling cost 32.50 RM per cubic meter and 146.25 RM per square meter.[11] The annual rent in these units ranged from 16.28 RM down to 14.64 RM per square meter, which translates into a weekly rent ranging from 17.75 RM in a two-story house to 15.96 RM in a four-story building. These rents, when compared to what people were able to pay, clearly explain the constant pressure to reduce the size of the dwellings and to build only in taller buildings.

Another set of calculations demonstrated essentially the same results. These showed that in Berlin the average net building costs of a standard one-and-one-half-room apartment were 6,156 RM; for a two-room apartment 7,695 RM; and for a two-and-one-half-room apartment 9,234 RM.[12] The weekly rents resulting from these costs were calculated as 11.50 RM, 14.38 RM, and 17.25 RM, respectively. Of course, it must be remembered that these costs resulted in part from the enhanced minimal standards of modern dwellings, such as the provision of private toilet facilities for each family. Each of these apartments had, in addition to the number of rooms mentioned, kitchen facilities and a separate small bathroom, which included both a tub and a toilet. Nevertheless, these rents, which were calculated on the basis of cost alone, still compared unfavorably to the amount average workers could afford to pay. The laconic contemporary comment was that "socially questionable conditions" were the unavoidable consequence.[13] In other words, many people still could not afford a decent dwelling.

Social awareness on the part of architects and their recognition of the crucial role of government in financing housing was exemplified by Ludwig Hilberseimer. He wrote,

> Every bit as important as the transformation of the production process is the transformation of the method of financing. Perhaps a more graduated system of public loans should be instituted, in order to adjust the price of apartments to the income of the renter, but without diminishing the quality of the dwelling.[14]

Certainly one of the most fundamental prerequisites for raising the sociocultural level of workers' housing was seen to be financing according to principles of the greatest good for the greatest number rather than the highest profit for the few. Thus, financing and the requisite degree of government support turned workers' housing into a political matter. Politics, pragmatism, and hardheaded economics played major roles in the advancement of housing. Designing an acceptable minimal dwelling was one aspect of this program.

# 6

# *Siedlungen* and *Wohnbauten*

## Introduction

The housing projects discussed in this chapter were chosen as being most representative of developments in Berlin from the First World War to just before the Nazi takeover in 1933. They represent the principal design philosophies for workers' housing in Berlin and include among them the most publicized settlements of the time. The selection is based on a desire to present a continuous narrative of progress toward the ambitious goals of planners, architects, and social reformers and to demonstrate how these goals were modified over time.

Everything presented here deserves the title of "public housing," since it was intended to satisfy the needs of a broad segment of the populace, was built by public benefit building corporations, and was supported by public funds. These public benefit corporations were sponsored by a broad array of organizations, ranging from small workers' cooperatives, through the blue and white collar labor unions, to companies seeking to house their own employees and various levels of government wanting to house civil servants, or to the municipality or state simply trying to relieve the housing crisis for the poor. One key characteristic all these building organizations had in common was that they were *gemeinnützig*, i.e., in the public interest rather than for profit. Speculation and profit-taking were to be eliminated; dividends were limited to five percent; housing was to be provided as a service, because society needed it.

It is my contention that this attitude of providing housing as a public service to the working class is the most important and the most impressive aspect of the housing revolution in Berlin. High social ideals were the key ingredients, and those organizations and architects closest to the labor unions went furthest in developing new concepts of housing for the masses. Thus the question of patronage emerges as an important issue for further study. To the extent that this question has been explored here, it is clear that GEHAG, the building corporation of the federation of labor unions, and therefore the one most committed to socialistic principles, was the patron commissioning the most progressive architecture. Organizations such as Primus, supported directly by the municipality under its Social Democratic administration, were very close to GEHAG in spirit.

GAGFAH, as mentioned earlier, represented a different type of clientele, had a more conservative approach, and favored traditional looking architecture. Housing organizations similar to GAGFAH, i.e., those sponsored by associations of salaried employees, civil servants, and other conservative groups, also tended toward more traditional architectural forms. In this latter category should be included the paternal, employer-sponsored building organizations, such as those formed by the Siemens corporation or the streetcar company. In the presentations of individual projects I have attempted to indicate patronage and its impact.

At the end of chapter 1, in defining the concept of *Siedlung*, I differentiated between *Klein-Siedlungen, Gross-Siedlungen,* and *Wohn-bauten,* with *Siedlung* implying the presence of gardens to be tilled, while *Wohnbauten* were simply residential buildings. While one primary distinction between large and small settlements was, of course, the number of units, the term *Gross-Siedlung* came by 1929 to have the special connotation of providing significant communal facilities, such as recreation areas and shops, central or district heating, communal laundry and ironing facilities, and daycare centers. Developments conceived and planned as communities, with provisions to encourage socializing and to make life easier—especially for mothers—are of greater inherent interest than mere agglomerations of dwellings. While this emphasis is best seen in the *Gross-Siedlungen* of 1929–30 (discussed in chapter 7), it was part of the design intent from the beginning.

Up to 1927 the garden city movement and a widespread back-to-nature enthusiasm provided an important basis for the planning of modern settlements. An important interchange of ideas concerning garden city concepts and low-density planning took place between Germany and England well before the First World War. Hermann Muthesius and Raymond Unwin served as links, as did family ties between the royal houses of the two countries (Kaiser Wilhelm II was Queen Victoria's "favorite grandson"). But the German Garden City Association—and especially its untiring leader Hans Kampffmeyer—was crucial in propagating garden city concepts in the 1920s. Related to this is the whole school of planning stemming from the teachings of Camillo Sitte. Periodicals, too, such as *Der Städtebau* and *Stadtbaukunst,* played important roles in disseminating ideas, as did important teachers, such as Theodor Fischer and Felix Genzmer. All of these influences are worthy of careful study and illumination.

By touching upon these important precedents and abstracting the important planning principles motivating German architects and reformers in the 1920s, I hope to have provided a key to understanding an aspect of modern architecture too often overlooked.

## Gartenstadt Staaken

It seems ironic that the first significant new housing in Berlin demonstrating enlightened socialistic principles should have been erected under the auspices of the imperial government during the First World War. Built in 1914–17 for workers in the Spandau munitions factory, *Gartenstadt Staaken*[1] was commissioned by the Ministry of the Interior and designed by Paul Schmitthenner (fig. 6). The ministry purchased the land, provided it with utilities, leased it to its own building cooperative at a mere two percent of the value, and also made funds for building available at low interest rates. It is only due to this direct government support that the settlement could be built at a time when all other housing construction was at a virtual standstill because of the war.

This *Gartenstadt* (really a garden suburb) was intended as a prototype, applying garden city principles to the design of workers' housing. It was a closed, unified settlement of low-rise buildings surrounded by agriculture and provided with ample gardens. One-third of the buildings were single-family, two-story row houses, each with its own attached garden, while the remainder consisted of two and four-family houses, also with attached gardens. The buildings were arranged on a pattern of gently curving streets about a central area containing church, school and market square. Streets and building lines deviated from the rectangular sufficiently to create closed vistas and intimate spaces in street and square: a carefully planned atmosphere of community and neighborliness (figs. 7, 8). Intimate contact with nature was fostered as part of this scheme to settle urban workers in the rural outskirts. Staaken thus provided an example of the housing amenities that could be supplied to the working class by benevolent paternalism. In site layout and building type it followed English prototypes and also related to the pre-war *Siedlungen* of the Krupp company in Essen, particularly the *Kolonie Alfredshof* and the *Siedlung Margaretenhöhe*.

## Siedlung an der Lentze Allee

Much closer to the central city and among the earliest post-war low-density workers' settlements was that on Lentze Allee.[2] Designed by Heinrich Schweitzer and built in 1920, this settlement is in an idyllic area which to the

Figure 6. *Gartenstadt Staaken*, commemorative graphic, 1917
An excellent revelation of the idyllic garden city concept popular among planners and reformers since the early years of the century. This graphic also foretells the intimate linkage between social propaganda and workers' housing during the 1920s. Translated it reads:

This city was built at a time
When a terrible war was raging.
This remember, those whose home it has become,
And stay true to the Fatherland.

(From a privately printed commemorative brochure)

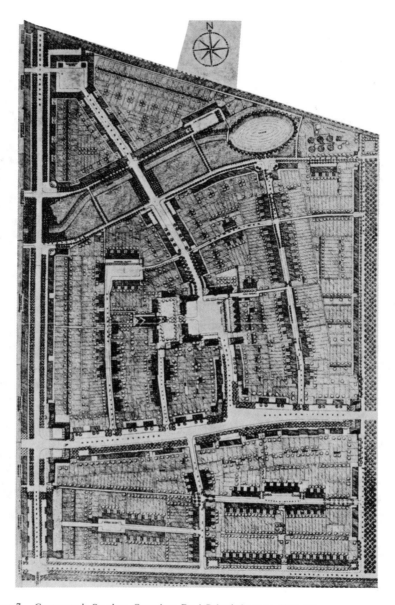

Figure 7.  *Gartenstadt Staaken,* Spandau, Paul Schmitthenner, 1914–17
Site plan. An emphasis on tillable family gardens and picturesque arrangement of
street spaces in the tradition of Camillo Sitte is apparent.
(*Wasmuth's Monatshefte für Baukunst,* III [1918/20], p. 198)

Figure 8. *Gartenstadt Staaken*, market square at the center of the complex
The intent to create a cohesive community with a clear identity of its own was
characteristic of the garden city movement and also of most siedlung planning in the 1920s.
(Photo: the author)

present day retains a semirural atmosphere in keeping with Hermann Jansen's 1909–10 development plan for Dahlem (fig. 9). Schweitzer's settlement uses a peripheral design scheme *(Randbebauung)*, then considered to be a direct application of the projected new building code. Continuous row houses were built around three edges of a large site, leaving much tillable land within for sizable residents' allotment gardens (fig. 10). "Back to the land" was the clear intention here, and the settlement has an almost traditional rural quality about it, including a North German vernacular style of half-timber, shingle and brick.

Everything is rudimentary and simple. Each dwelling in the row houses consists of two rooms up and two rooms down, one each front and back (fig. 11). The rural nature of the settlement goes so far as to include an attached shed for animal husbandry at the back of each unit. Between the all-purpose living-kitchen *(Wohnküche)* and this shed are the scullery and laundry *(Spüle und Waschküche)*. The bathroom is on the second floor above the scullery. This arrangement of living-kitchen with separate scullery, although repeated by Walter Gropius as late as 1926 in his *Dessau-Törten Siedlung*, did not gain popular acceptance in Germany. The *Siedlung an der Lentze Allee*, however, was among the few settlements built in the period just after the war and provided an example for the construction of simple dwellings in close relationship to the earth. Since it was commissioned by the *Kommission zur Aufteilung der Domäne Dahlem*, a government planning agency, and was intended for employees of the municipal government, it—like Staaken—must be considered as a type of paternal "company housing" for bureaucrats.

### Siedlung Lindenhof

A more richly varied and larger development of a related peripheral type was also built shortly after the war by Martin Wagner, then municipal building councilor *(Stadtbaurat)* for the borough of Schöneberg (See figs. 12–14). Lindenhof was built in 1919–20 for the borough itself.[3] It consisted of one, two, and three-room apartments with living-kitchens, like those on Lentze Allee. Each apartment had a garden of at least 100 square meters, which was expected to be tilled. The site was particularly advantageous for a *Siedlung* intended to restore contact with nature, since it already included two ponds and a stand of mature linden trees. Wagner's esthetic treatment of the houses was even more rudimentary than Schweitzer's: starkly simple forms and no ornament. The principal amenities were the site itself and the interesting spatial relationships achieved through site layout. The design enclosed the pond, the trees and the gardens with peripheral row houses and divided the site with a curving diagonal spine composed of a street and flanking buildings, which led from Bruno Taut's curiously monumental dormitory for single men

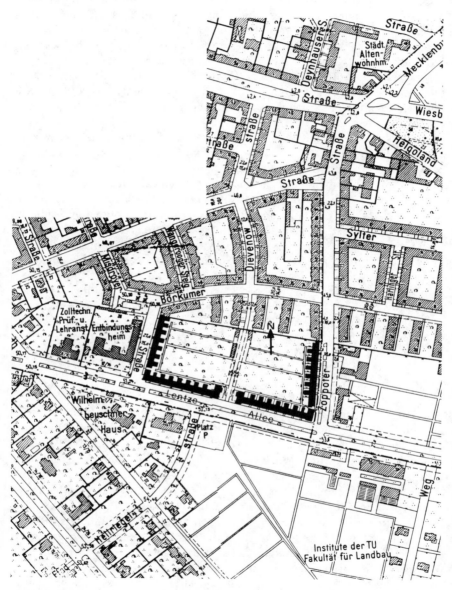

Figure 9. *Siedlung an der Lentze Allee,* Berlin-Wilmersdorf, Heinrich Schweitzer, 1920
Site plan.
(Courtesy Senator für Bau- und Wohnungswesen)

Figure 10.  *Siedlung an der Lentze Allee*
    View of the peripheral construction along Lentze Allee (right) and Zoppoter
    Strasse (right)
    (*40 Jahre Berlinische Bodengesellschaft*, p. 72)

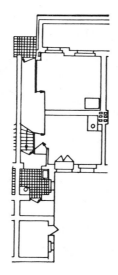

Figure 11.  *Siedlung an der Lentze Allee*
    Plan at ground level, showing the scullery and attached shed for small animal
    husbandry.
    (*Stadtbaukunst alter und neuer Zeit*, II [1921], p. 217. Courtesy Bernd
    Feuerherd)

Figure 12. *Siedlung Lindenhof*, Berlin-Schöneberg, Martin Wagner, 1919–20
Aerial view. Bachelors' Billet at the northeast corner of the settlement is at the top of the photo.
(Wolf, *Wohnung und Siedlung*, p. 211)

Figure 13.  Bachelors' Billet, *Siedlung Lindenhof*, Bruno Taut, 1919–20
View from the garden side, terminating in a vista at the northeast corner of the siedlung.
(Gut, *Wohnungsneubau in Deutschland*, p. 567)

Figure 14.  *Siedlung Lindenhof*
View of row-house along the south side of the pond.
(Photo: the author)

to a village square at the center of the development. The arrangement of points of view and vistas is similar to Staaken and exemplifies principles of composition promulgated in *Der Städtebau* since 1904.[4]

Bruno Taut had already designed the bachelors' billet for this settlement in 1918.[5] The incorporation of a home for single men reflects the fact that one of the most detrimental influences on family life in Germany during the early twentieth century was the widespread practice—born of economic necessity—of subletting parts of rooms—lamentably, however, often only the shared use of a bed—to strangers. Part of the plan at Lindenhof was thus to relieve family life of the disruptive social effects of subtenants and to provide unmarried workers with their own quarters and facilities for socializing.

It is an interesting footnote that the Lindenhof design had gone so far in correcting the overcrowding of typical workers' housing that the site density of this project was later considered to be excessively low. During rebuilding in the 1950s, additional housing was added to bring the density up to contemporary standards for urban areas.

### Siedlung Tempelhofer Feld

Development plans for this area had already aroused heated debate before the war, so that when the project was finally built according to the designs of Fritz Bräuning,[6] building councilor for the borough of Tempelhof, it was reported and followed with great interest. The land had previously been part of the military exercise grounds for the Berlin garrison, and, in a series of events clouded by corruption among high military and state officials, this large area within the city had almost fallen into the hands of speculators. Plans had been drawn up to develop it on the old pattern of high-density five-story rental barracks, a plan which was opposed by the revolutionary government after the war, when the decision was made to develop the area as a model *Siedlung* to demonstrate the principles of garden settlements and to provide housing for returning war veterans.

The succession of plans (figs. 15–17) drawn up for this area provides fascinating insights, starting with the first, which shows a typical late nineteenth-century plan of grand avenues and star intersections. At first glance, this plan would seem to provide picturesque variety in its curved and broken street patterns. Yet the principal considerations are clearly outmoded concepts of monumentality: an architecture of facades. The space behind these facades—all the space within the blocks—is cross-hatched as if it might as well be one solid mass, revealing a disregard for the character of the dwellings and the light or air which might reach them. Other obvious disadvantages of such plans, including the irregular street intersections and angularly shaped building plots, had been revealed by Camillo Sitte well before the turn of the century; they were generally recognized as undesirable.

Figure 15. *Siedlung Tempelhofer Feld,* Berlin-Tempelhof, Fritz Bräuning, 1924–28
Original plan for high-density development of the site, with grand boulevards
and star intersections; however all of the area for housing is shown shaded, as if
conceived a solid mass.
(*40 Jahre Berlinische Bodengesellschaft,* p. 32)

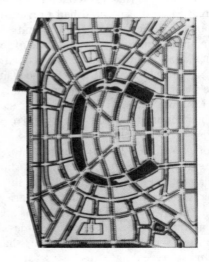

Figure 16. *Siedlung Tempelhofer Feld*
Improved high-density plan for the site, with a substantial strip-park
incorporated into the design.
(*40 Jahre Berlinische Bodengesellschaft,* p. 33)

Figure 17.  *Siedlung Tempelhofer Feld*
Bräuning's low-density garden settlement plan for the site (houses drawn black),
with higher density blocks on the periphery, including those at the east by
Eduard Jobst Siedler.
(Johannes, *Neues Bauen in Berlin,* p. 62)

Figure 18.  *Siedlung Tempelhofer Feld*
Aerial view of the settlement from the southeast, with the arched entry to the
complex in the foreground.
(Heilig, *Stadt- und Landbaukunde,* p. 80)

Figure 19.  *Siedlung Tempelhofer Feld*
View of the arched entry to the complex through a peripheral block at the southeast.
(Schmidt and Ebel, *Wohnungsneubau der Nachkriegszeit in Deutschland,* p. 174)

Figure 20.  *Siedlung Tempelhofer Feld*
Characteristic semi-detached dwellings by Bräuning on the *Bundesring.* These were criticized by Bruno Taut for their figurative ornament and layout, which required some parties to enter their dwellings through the gardens.
(Wolf, *Wohnung und Siedlung,* p. 212)

Figure 21. *Siedlung Tempelhofer Feld*
Partial site plan showing the individual gardens of the semi-detached dwellings and the taller peripheral apartment blocks to the south and east.
(*40 Jahre Berlinische Bodengesellschaft,* p. 80.)

Figure 22. *Siedlung Tempelhofer Feld,* Eduard Jobst Siedler, 1925–28
Apartment blocks along the east periphery. These taller blocks enclose and shelter the garden settlement from the main traffic artery and the new airport to the east.
(Gut, *Wohnungsneubau in Deutschland,* p. 536)

A later plan for this area of the *Tempelhofer Feld* shows a series of concentric rings, including a band of green, combined with radiating avenues and a central monumental square. Here too, the basic concern is with formal streets and facades around closed blocks. While seemingly only a street plan, with no indications of housing type, the implication is that high-density housing more or less fills the voids: a clear indication of speculative planning, only marginally better than average because of its varied street pattern and interesting use of greenery.

This second plan is the one the private development corporation had proposed using, covering the site with five-story rental barracks. The curving arc of streets was primarily the result of containment of the site to the west and south by railroad tracks. The resemblance of this intermediate street layout to the one finally used indicates that some streets had already been established when Bräuning and the specially formed building company, the *Gemeinnützige Tempelhofer Feld Heimstätten Gesellschaft,* took over.

Bräuning's plan consisted primarily of two and three-family detached houses and row houses arranged with emphasis on curving streets, closed vistas, and the creation of intimately scaled squares. Great care was taken to limit through traffic to a minimum and to provide each family with its own garden adjacent to its dwelling. Taller buildings were designed for the periphery to give a sense of enclosure and formal definition to the total complex. The emphasis placed on the esthetics of spatial design is especially clear at the southeast corner of the *Siedlung,* where a great, monumental forecourt and entrance invited people in through the arched entry onto the main circular road of the settlement. This archway also framed a picturesque vista of semi-detached houses curving into the distance. The gazebo over the central axis of the archway, the free-standing sculptured putti, and the little figurative plaques on the facades of various buildings demonstrated a somewhat quaint and outmoded concern for ornament. Yet the generous spaciousness of this settlement, its gardens, and its sensitive spatial composition all make a very attractive ensemble.

As might be expected, however, the quaintly bourgeois-traditional or Biedermeier characteristics of Bräuning's project did not go uncriticized by Bruno Taut, who scathingly commented about the seemingly large detached houses that looked like villas but were actually duplexes or triplexes linked by garden walls, "Herr Biedermeier holds himself aloof from his neighbors, yet shares his house with two other parties. They must use the servants' entrance in the garden wall for access to their apartments. As a consolation there are sweet cherubs and flowers on the house."[7]

The tall building blocks bordering the *Siedlung Tempelhofer Feld* to the east, along the major street leading to the heart of Berlin, form an example of the principle of surrounding a spacious garden settlement with a wall of taller housing.[8] In this case, the taller peripheral housing serves not only as protection from a major traffic artery (Berliner Strasse, today Tempelhofer Damm), but also from the new airport built in the 1920s on the larger part of the *Tempelhofer Feld* to the east. (Tempelhof remained the principal airport of West Berlin until the 1970s and is still the airport of the American garrison.) These peripheral buildings were designed by Eduard Jobst Siedler, professor at the *Technische Hochschule* in Charlottenburg, chief administrator of the German Architects' Association *(Bund Deutscher Architekten)*, and editor of its professional journal, *Die Baugilde*. Siedler's special system, quite different from the norm for apartment buildings, consisted of two parallel bands of dwellings separated by a narrow courtyard, with staircases connecting the two bands. This was intended to save building expenses in low-density housing projects by concentrating dwellings on a small fraction of the site, building upward rather than outward, and thus freeing a large portion of the site for gardens.[9] At Tempelhof, however, Siedler's buildings served simply to provide a higher-density band around a low-density core.

### *Siedlung Siemensstadt*

Hans Hertlein was responsible for creating the architectural image associated with the major electrical manufacturer, Siemens & Halske, in the vast area called Siemens City (Siemensstadt),[10] consisting of parts of the boroughs of Charlottenburg and Spandau in the northwestern part of Greater Berlin (figs. 23–25). Hertlein, as director of the building department of the entire Siemens concern, designed administrative and factory buildings not only in Berlin but in Cologne, Nuremberg, and in other parts of the world, including Buenos Aires. In Siemensstadt, besides this early workers' settlement, he also did the *Siedlung Heimat* at the end of the decade (see chapter 7); both are company housing for the *Wohnungsgesellschaft Siemensstadt*. The first *Siedlung* was built between 1922 and 1928 according to what we should now perhaps call garden-suburb principles: picturesque layout to create vistas and interesting street spaces, and a rowhouse arrangement with attached subsistence gardens surrounded by taller apartment buildings designed to give a sense of containment and unity.

We now recognize the Sittesque qualities of Raps Strasse, curving and contained, with houses moved forward or backward or off axis to contract, expand and articulate spaces. Entrances to the settlement, corners, and nodal points all receive special treatment. Formal elements such as gables relate to each other across these spaces, and streets are curved or angled to provide visual accents and to close vistas in the same manner we have seen employed by Bräuning at Tempelhof, Wagner at Lindenhof, and Schmitthenner at Staaken. Of course, the evocation of vernacular and village character is also

Figure 23.  *Siedlung Siemensstadt,* Spandau, Hans Hertlein, 1922–28
Arched entry at the north end of Raps Strasse. Site planning in this settlement,
too, is based on the picturesque school influenced by Camillo Sitte.
(Hertlein, *Siemensbauten,* p. 106–21)

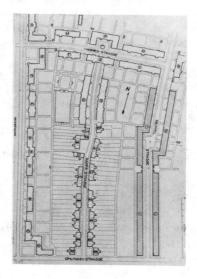

Figure 24.  *Siedlung Siemensstadt*
View north from the southern end of Raps Strasse.
(Hertlein, *Siemensbauten,* p. 106–21)

Figure 25. *Siedlung Siemensstadt*
Site plan, including shaded additions of 1919–30.
(Hertlein, *Siemensbauten*, p. 106–21)

similar and was part of the mythos of returning the industrial workers to healthful and invigorating contact with the earth.

It is instructive to "walk through" the spatial sequence to realize just how remarkably sensitive the space planning of these—after all—low-cost workers' housing settlements was. Approaching Raps Strasse from the south, one crosses the western end of *Jungfernheide* (Maiden's Heath) park toward houses clearly arranged to form an entrance. While the houses are quite simple in shape and traditional in appearance, their alignment is varied to avoid monotony. One immediately notices a gabled and arcaded facade terminating the vista, which, upon approach, reveals itself as a nodal point—little more than a jog in the road—but clearly a kind of village center at which convenience shopping is located. Beyond this point the street continues northward in a slight curve to the next vista *(Blickpunkt),* where the enclosing building band, accented by the axial clock tower above, arches over the street, which passes beneath and terminates in the forecourt of a U-shaped dwelling block across Harries Strasse. This concern for sequential spatial experience is seen throughout. Even the external bands of buildings do not create the monotonous sensation of a continuous wall, but are arranged to create courts and other articulated spatial units. The net effect is one of interest and identifiability, clearly qualities likely to stimulate a sense of community among residents.

We should note that all of the examples presented so far were paternalistic housing projects of one sort or another; i.e., a company or government agency had housing built for its own employees. There is an interesting correlation in that all of the designs were conservative and traditional, planned in accordance with concepts of low-density, picturesque settlement types established prior to the First World War.

### Siedlung Heidehof

Another of the peripheral settlements of the early twenties which placed great emphasis on quiet, enclosed spaces is *Siedlung Heidehof.*[11] Built in 1923–24 for a civil servants' *Beamten-Wohnungsbau-Verein* by Paul Mebes and Paul Emmerich, this settlement is located on Potsdamer Chaussee in southwestern Berlin. Here again the vernacular tradition was used along with sensitive site planning to create contained spaces with simple, unadorned row houses. The layout creates a village square, a quiet, domestic island in a wooded grove (figs. 26, 27). Traffic is kept at a distance and houses are surrounded with trees and gardens. These gardens appear as extended living spaces, because the arrangement of the buildings coupled with the trees gives them a sense of containment and shelter. The dwelling plans were of a standard type,

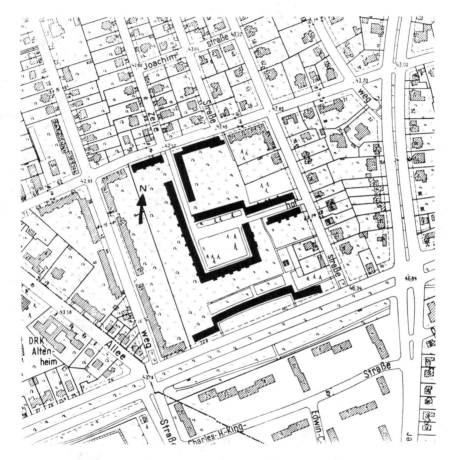

Figure 26. *Siedlung Heidehof,* Zehlendorf, Mebes & Emmerich, 1923–24
Site plan. Simple vernacular brick style is here combined with picturesque
planning to create a sense of tradition and containment.
(Courtesy Senator für Bau- und Wohnungswesen)

Figure 27. *Siedlung Heidehof*
View into the central court.
(Schallenberger, *Der Wohnungsneubau in Berlin*, p. 10)

rudimentary and compact; yet the vernacular qualities—red brick walls and gables, steeply pitched roofs, and the sense of containment—achieve a traditional coziness *(Gemütlichkeit)* which expresses the conserving spirit of historic preservation *(Heimatschutz)* often associated with German associations of civil servants.

## Siedlung Schillerpark

Bruno Taut's relatively early *Siedlung,*[12] adjoining Schiller Park in Reinickendorf, was designed just after he had given up his position as *Stadtbaurat* in Magdeburg to resume private practice in Berlin. In this variation on the peripheral plan he utilized straight blocks along the street fronts, but allowed courtyards and street spaces to merge by opening up the corners of the blocks (fig. 28). One of the most striking features of this complex is its rich use of colors, textures and surface patterns, continuing Taut's Magdeburg crusade for a colorful city *(die bunte Stadt)* but with other means. Certainly one might consider that Taut's *Schillerpark* achieved a more successful use of color than in Magdeburg, where he used wall surfaces as easels for abstract designs. Throughout the 1920s he was to further develop his ideas of how best to brighten cities through color; here his choice was for the inherent color contrasts of red brick and stucco and the employment of striking shadow effects, achieved by advance and recession in balconies, loggias, stair towers, or cantilevered planes. The Schillerpark houses develop interesting variations on these architectural themes. In fact, the variations of visual effect suggest a spirit of experimentation.

Furthermore, the complexity and intricacy of the dwelling plans seem to be the result of Taut's desire to achieve striking exterior effects through balconies—or rather loggias *(Lauben)*—with their shadow effects. Apparently formalistic considerations played a major role, since the floor plans are no improvement over the standard then in use. The very use of the three-span type *(Dreispännertyp),* with three apartments opening from each landing, was already considered outmoded and undesirable, because of its lack of two-sided exposure and its lack of cross-ventilation for the central apartment.

The *Siedlung Schillerpark* is particularly interesting in regard to patronage, since it is one of the first settlements directly linked to the socialist labor unions and the first to have a strikingly non-traditional appearance. It was constructed by the socialized building trades *(Bauhütte Berlin)* in which Martin Wagner was so influential, and thus continues the fruitful relationship between Wagner and Bruno Taut which began at Lindenhof and was to make its mark across Berlin during the remainder of the decade.

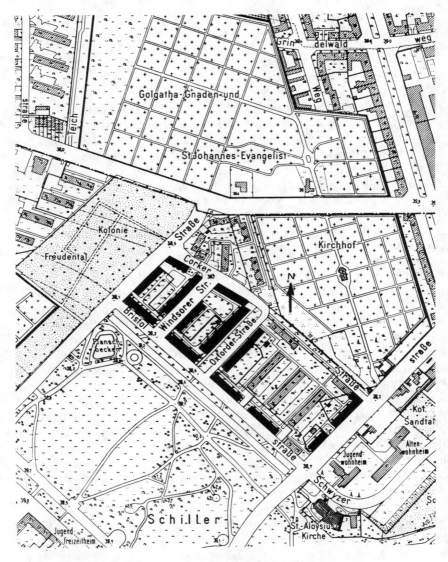

Figure 28. *Siedlung Schillerpark,* Berlin-Wedding, Bruno Taut, 1923–24 and 1928
Site plan, with modifications of the 1950s. A peripheral plan was here opened at
several points.
(Courtesy Senator für Bau- und Wohnungswesen)

Figure 29. *Siedlung Schillerpark*
View into Bristol Strasse of flat-roofed, red-brick apartment buildings of the three-span type.
(Schmidt and Ebel, *Wohnungsneubau der Nachkriegszeit*, p. 196)

Figure 30. *Siedlung Schillerpark*
Apartment plan, showing the arrangement of three dwellings around one
landing; a type generally out of favor in Berlin during the 1920s.
(Schallenberger, *Wohnungsneubau in Berlin*, p. 6)

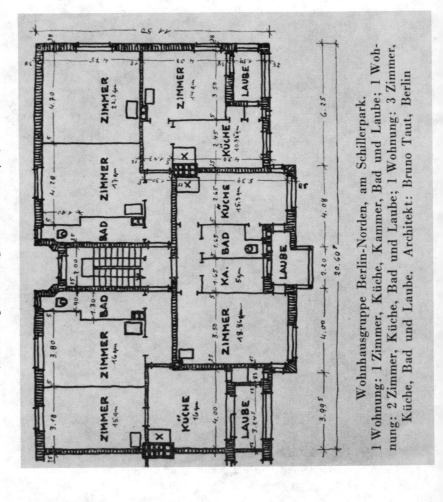

Wohnhausgruppe Berlin-Norden, am Schillerpark.
1 Wohnung: 1 Zimmer, Küche, Kammer, Bad und Laube; 1 Wohnung: 2 Zimmer, Küche, Bad und Laube; 1 Wohnung: 3 Zimmer,
Küche, Bad und Laube. Architekt: Bruno Taut, Berlin

One is immediately aware of a different approach to architecture and planning, compared to everything seen in the conservative projects considered above. Here one senses the bold statement of new site planning ideas and building forms, a forcefulness of expression, drawing attention to itself as something revolutionary. The preference for flat roofs, straight lines, and right angles is symptomatic of the will to express the social spirit of a new age.

## Siedlung Ceciliengärten

By contrast to Schillerpark we might consider an interesting, yet somewhat anachronistic housing development built in Berlin in the mid-twenties. The *Siedlung Ceciliengärten*[13] in Schöneberg, on which Paul Wolf as planner and Heinz Lassen as architect collaborated, was built as company housing for the Berlin transit corporation by the *Gemeinnützige Heimstätten-Baugesellschaft der Berliner Strassenbahn*. The site plan was an old one, devised in 1910–14, revived for construction beginning in 1924 (fig. 31). Nevertheless, within the realm of traditional, monumental form language and high density building, the evils of rental barracks housing were eliminated through careful site planning and major revision of the nineteenth-century system of building monumental streets and neglecting what lay behind the facades.

From 1910 to 1914 Paul Wolf held the position of borough building councilor *(Magistratsbaurat)* in Schöneberg and headed its office of urban expansion. During this period he prepared the initial proposal for Ceciliengärten; and, in his book *City Planning: The Form Problem of the City in the Past and in the Future,* referred to this design to demonstrate the importance of administrative diplomacy in achieving better urban planning.[14] Since the existing urban plan had placed its emphasis on monumental facades, imposing streets, and useless angular intersections, it had taken great negotiating skill as well as sensitive design to transform the plan into something more positive.

Under the old assumption that eighty to ninety percent of the land between the streets would be built upon, there were no provisions for gardens or greenery of any sort. Wolf took pride in the fact that negotiations between the municipality and the land developers *(Terrain-Gesellschaft)* finally resulted in the adoption of a remarkably different plan, which called for the strong differentiation of streets, distinguishing sharply between residential and traffic streets. Thus what would have been the principal street running through the development was transformed into a public park, and large interior courtyards could become community park spaces, allowing all apartments to be oriented toward quiet, green enclosures (fig. 32). It is all the more remarkable that such important spatial amenities should have been achieved through design alone, since the population density and the rate of

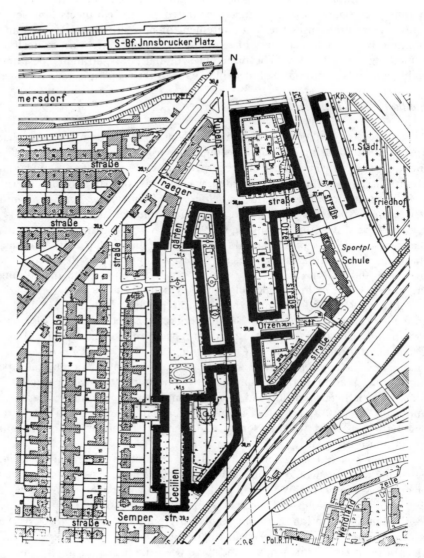

Figure 31. *Siedlung Ceciliengärten,* Berlin-Schöneberg, Paul Wolf (planner) and Heinz Lassen (architect), 1924–28
Site plan. Through careful planning and differentiation of street spaces a high-density settlement was created which provided generous exposure of all units to open green spaces.
(Courtesy Senator für Bau- und Wohnungswesen)

Figure 32. *Siedlung Ceciliengärten*
View toward the north in the largest park-like space.

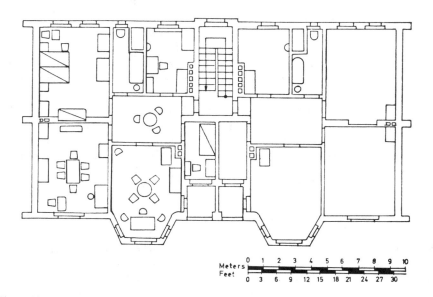

Meters 0 1 2 3 4 5 6 7 8 9 10
Feet 0 3 6 9 12 15 18 21 24 27 30

Figure 33. *Siedlung Ceciliengärten*
Typical three-and-one-half room apartment plan of a size much larger than what was to become standard later in the decade. This was the plan Alexander Klein used to demonstrate the weaknesses of normal dwelling layouts of the time. (Courtesy Bernd Feuerherd)

financial return to the developer remained the same as under the old system. One would have thought that precisely the distinction between the old, higher densities and the lower ones of the 1920s, and between the old building heights and the new, were the qualities that separated advanced housing of the twenties from what had come before, but here we see what great social benefits could be achieved simply through imaginative site planning alone.

Ideally, as envisioned by the housing reformers, two-thirds of all new housing construction in Berlin would have consisted of low-density, low-rise developments. That ideal was never achieved. In fact, the actual percentages more than reversed the ideal: almost three-quarters of all housing built in Berlin in the years 1924–26 consisted of taller buildings, four or five stories, with continued high densities. The low-density garden settlements were clearly a small minority.

The apartment plans in Ceciliengärten were of a type frequently used in Berlin, with rooms clustered around an entrance hall *(Diele;* fig. 33). A few years later the shortcomings and inefficiencies of such layouts were demonstrated by Alexander Klein with his method of graphic analysis, as we have seen in chapter 4. It should be recognized that, while the apartments at Ceciliengärten had a spaciousness that would soon be considered impossibly lavish, it was Klein's analytical system which provided not only more desirable alternatives in similar sizes, but which also provided the means by which much smaller yet still very attractive floor plans could be devised.

At Ceciliengärten the elimination of back and side buildings, the exposure of each apartment at both sides of the building, and the generous spacing of blocks to create interior parks, although major improvements over the old rental barracks system, represented the realization of *pre-war* advances in planning thought. The long extension of this site in a north-south direction, however, provided an opportunity for giving most of the units the desired east-west orientation that became one of the hallmarks of the twenties. Looking at the site plan of Ceciliengärten, one can sense the coming of the long parallel rows separated by bands of greenery, a style which was to be characteristic of the end of the decade.

### Gross-Siedlung Britz (Hufeisen Siedlung)

Undoubtedly the most famous of the earlier workers' housing projects in Berlin in the twenties was that known as the *Hufeisen* (horseshoe) *Siedlung,* [15] so called because of the form of its central group of buildings (figs. 34–38). It was built in the part of the borough of Neukölln known as Britz in the years 1925–26 for GEHAG, the building corporation of the blue collar trade unions, by Bruno Taut in collaboration with Martin Wagner. Although principal

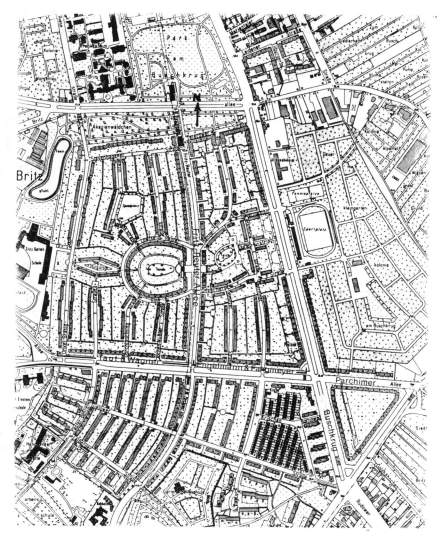

Figure 34. *Gross-Siedlung Britz (Hufeisen Siedlung),* Neukölln, Bruno Taut and Martin Wagner, 1925–26
Site plan. Mainly two-story row-houses, with three-story apartments forming the horseshoe and enclosing the settlement on the north, east and south. The DEGEWO portion of the *Gross-Siedlung Britz* is directly across Fritz Reuter Allee to the east.
(Courtesy Senator für Bau- und Wohnungswesen)

Figure 35.  *Gross-Siedlung Britz (Hufeisen Siedlung)*
Construction photo: entrance to the Hufeisen from within, with communal meeting spaces at the center.
(Photo: Arthur Köster. Courtesy Akademie der Künste)

Figure 36. *Gross-Siedlung Britz (Hufeisen Siedlung)*
Construction photo: exterior of the Hufeisen. View from a street of two-story row-houses.
(Photo: Arthur Köster. Courtesy Akademie der Künste)

Figure 37. *Gross-Siedlung Britz (Hufeisen Siedlung)*
Designed sense of containment in a street of row-houses. View south toward Parchimer Allee.
(Photo: Arthur Köster. Courtesy Akademie der Künste)

Figure 38. *Gross-Siedlung Britz (Hufeisen Siedlung)*
Modern, efficient kitchen with built-ins in a typical apartment. View in through the open window.
(Photo: Arthur Köster. Courtesy Akademie der Künste)

credit for the project is usually given to Taut, Wagner was responsible for planning the layout of the settlement as well as designing the northernmost building in it.

The development consisted primarily of two-story rowhouses, many of which were arranged in a generally north-south direction. The early plan uses the principle of gradation by enclosing the project to the north and east and surrounding the central pond and community park space with three-story apartment buildings. As executed, the southern perimeter of the development was also defined as an enclosing band of three-story buildings.

These slightly taller enclosing bands may be considered three-story, six-family rowhouses, since all are through-units of the two-span type. The buildings incorporate convenience shopping and community facilities, including a cafe and terrace restaurant at the entrance to the horseshoe. Taut paid careful attention to the formal aspects of this entrance area especially, in order to emphasize its function as communal focal point and frame for a generous community recreation space, creating an unusual balance between inviting openness and a very clear expression of containment. Visual unity and identification with other parts of this *Siedlung* are also major concerns.

The creation of such an unusually fine community space—all the more striking today now that the greenery Taut planted has grown up around the pond—is an important achievement of the *Hufeisen Siedlung*. This more than counterbalances the fact that one-third of the apartments on the horseshoe have their balconies facing north.

Exits from the horseshoe other than the main one were expressed in red brick, achieving clarity without sacrificing spatial containment. Furthermore, the loggias in this containing surface keep it from reading as a solid wall, providing instead an interesting sculptural play between solid and void, light and shadow. Along Fritz Reuter Allee (then *Grüner Ring*) on the eastern perimeter of the complex, on the other hand, Taut employed a fortress-like protective closure of peripheral buildings, apparently feeling that surface treatment should vary in accordance with expressive intentions.

Yet Taut's emphasis on these various formal elements reveals not only a sensitivity to visual effects but also a basically formalistic approach, which could—and did—have rather impractical results. Elements reminiscent of the early work of Frank Lloyd Wright—which had been published in Berlin in the Wasmuth monograph of 1910—abound, e.g., continuity of surfaces around corners, dramatically cantilevered rectangular planes, and the crisp rectangular termination of forms. Such formalistic devices—particularly when they resulted in the elimination of drip moldings at the tops of walls on flat-roofed buildings—had already allowed water damage in the first year these buildings stood.[16]

The single-family rowhouses, on the other hand, had pitched, overhanging roofs and were designed to play an entirely different role in the complex. With the exception of the stylized rectangular slabs over the entrances, which had no pitch and made no provision for protecting the entrances from dripping water, the designs of the rowhouses were simple and straightforward. Here an intimate scale, striking use of local color, and the careful placement—or displacement—of the buildings in relationship to each other worked together to create distinctive street spaces in the area beyond the horseshoe. The means—derived from Sitte and Unwin—of bending streets and varying setbacks were skillfully used by Taut to achieve an atmosphere of small, discrete neighborhood units within the settlement; yet this feeling of intimacy and identifiability was accomplished using a consistent system of standard types. The planning here was intended to exemplify the possibility of applying standardized construction on a large scale while still achieving varied and interesting spaces, and also responding to the site's topography.

Taut intended to express his enthusiasm for the socially coherent mass of workers and felt that the grouping of similar elements in a workers' settlement would demonstrate this enthusiasm for the collective as a vital entity, infusing the whole project with the spirit of a new social order. Concerning the design of *Siedlungen* as an expression of the collective spirit, Bruno Taut summarized his attitude as follows:

> The uniformly pitched roofs and the use of color in the spirit of a melodious interaction in the whole achieve a supreme harmony. These are the unmistakable signs of truly collective building, building which captures the sense of totality and which is the most beautiful expression of a supra-personal sensitivity.[17]

Although one may question Taut's rhetoric, and although one may wonder how—according to the logic of his own terms—he could deny any of the other *Siedlungen* the quality of expressing the collective, these words do serve to show his strong social consciousness and also to explain the symbolism of the form language he employed. Strikingly bold, purist shapes and vivid colors combined with white were to him symbols of a new social order and of a desire to break away from the old.

Taut's strong social convictions, combined with his adherence to these symbols, led him to severely criticize his neighbors to the east, the DEGEWO portion of the *Gross-Siedlung Britz* designed by Engelmann and Fangmeyer. In dwelling plans and in the basic principles of spatial arrangement, the two portions of this *Gross-Siedlung* are actually closely related to each other and to the German city planning traditions of the early twentieth century. The associations of the form languages chosen, however, were effective signs saying "radical modernism" on the one hand and "conservative traditionalism" on the other.

## DEGEWO Portion of the *Gross-Siedlung Britz*

An interesting example of the precepts characterizing advanced settlement design in the Berlin of the mid-1920s is that portion of the *Gross-Siedlung Britz*[18] north of Parchimer Allee (then called Kirsch Allee for the cherry trees which still attract many visitors each spring) and across Fritz Reuter Allee (then *Grüner Ring*), east of the *Hufeisen Siedlung* (fig. 39). This settlement, designed by the team of Ernst Engelmann and E. Fangmeyer and built for DEGEWO *(Deutsche Gesellschaft zur Förderung des Wohnungsbaues)* in the years 1925–26, differs dramatically from Taut and Wagner's work in the stylistic treatment of building exteriors. It is this aspect, and—one senses— perhaps some personal acrimony, that must have motivated Taut to consign Engelmann and Fangmeyer's work to oblivion in his book *Bauen: der neue Wohnbau,* where he went so far as to draw enormous X's over their portions of the *Gross-Siedlung* in aerial photos intended to show his own work.

The plan of Engelmann and Fangmeyer's project makes the layout principles quite apparent. Here, once again, we see the concept of gradation applied in surrounding grouped lower buildings by a taller, three-story band of apartment houses, while a depression containing a pond—similar to that which gave Taut his justification for the horseshoe arrangement—was utilized by Engelmann and Fangmeyer as the center of a more intimately scaled park space in the center of their complex. About 1000 dwelling units were provided here, just as across the street, apartments in the three-story peripheral buildings and single-family units in two-story rowhouses, each of which had its own substantial adjoining garden. In keeping with normal practice, while the apartment dwellers were not provided with their own gardens, they had community lawns adjacent to their buildings, and these were visually extended by the expanses of private allotments.

The impression conveyed by the site planning is a romantic grouping based on concepts of curved streets and closed vistas, i.e., again the tradition of Sitte and Unwin. Yet the design is not all crooked roads and impractical romanticism, which is the way Sitte was frequently misinterpreted. Rather, one notices a consistent emphasis on an east-west exposure for most dwelling units, with the principal streets and the majority of the buildings running generally north-south. There was also careful economy in downscaling internal access streets—again as Taut and Wagner did—in order to restrict through traffic, reduce the cost of infrastructure, and make the entire settlement into a series of quiet spaces.

Visually as well, these spaces were enclosed and defined to emphasize the human scale and a sense of intimacy. Although the design of individual units was spartan in its simplicity, stepped gables, varying setbacks of the houses, and even an occasional turret were used to define spaces and to emphasize a

Figure 39. *Gross-Siedlung Britz, DEGEWO portion,* Neukölln, Engelmann & Fangmeyer, 1925-26
Contemporary but competing settlement across Fritz Reuter Allee from Taut and Wagner's Hufeisen. Although based upon the same planning principals and also using gradation to surround two-story row-houses with three-story apartment buildings, the DEGEWO portion is overtly conservative and traditional in its form language, while the GEHAG portion is boldly modern. Aerial photo from the northeast showing similarity of planning in the two portions. DEGEWO portion in the foreground, GEHAG portion beyond.

sense of tradition. This can be seen particularly well at what appears to be a forked intersection just north of the pond area. Actually simply a bend in the road transformed into a miniature square by the arrangement of the buildings (as Hertlein had done at Siemensstadt), the space here is also entered by a footpath up a flight of stairs from the east. Approaching from any of three directions, one is confronted by a closed vista and a set of gables. By means of such slight adjustments of street axes and the orientation and placement of buildings, the architects demonstrated their sensitivity to containment, identifiability and intimacy in residential planning. They showed one way in which limited means can be put to effective use in creating a pleasant living environment.

### Wohnbauten Weser-, Werra-, Inn-Strasse

One of the more successful solutions to the problem of higher density housing closer to the urban core was provided by Paul Mebes and Paul Emmerich in the borough of Neukölln on the full block bounded by Weser, Werra, Inn, and Rosegger Street for the *Beamten-Wohnungsbauverein Neukölln*[19] (figs. 40–42). The project was begun in 1925. Paul Mebes was a member of the board of directors of this long established building association (founded 1900) for government clerks and officials. As the association's architect, he had been building rather pleasant housing developments, utilizing traditional form language and providing far more than the usual amenities of space—especially gardens—for this group of Berlin civil servants since shortly after the turn of the century.[20]

The large block in Neukölln, treated as an esthetically and functionally unified entity, was designed in recognition of the persisting need for higher density building closer to the urban core. In spite of the theorists' great enthusiasm for the merits of single-family dwellings with adjoining gardens in low-density settlements as the ideal workers' housing, it was apparent that in older, built-up areas, along existing wide streets, and for in-fill projects in older neighborhoods, the multistory apartment block still had an important role to play. However, as we shall see, this particular block had virtually nothing in common with the old rental barracks, except that both were large and both enclosed the site by flanking the streets with tall facades.

A most striking feature of this block is its lavish sense of openness within the courtyards. Toward the outside there is a striking effect of unity and clarity expressed in the economical, yet sensitively detailed unified street fronts. W.C. Behrendt considered the treatment of masses, the detailing and proportioning, and the handling of form in this block as accomplishments on the level of Schinkel, the grand ancestor of all Berlin architects.[21]

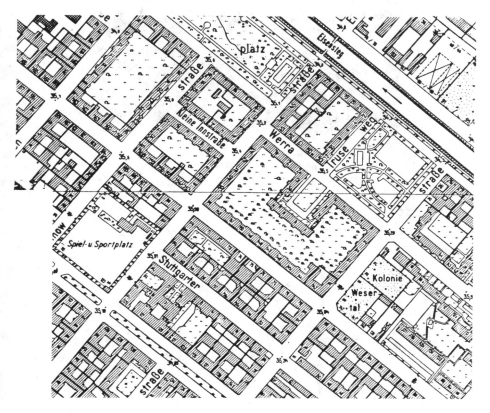

Figure 40. *Wohnbauten Weser-, Werra-, Inn-Strasse,* Neukölln, Mebes & Emmerich,
1924–25
Site plan. Higher density housing in an urban setting, but incorporating large,
semi-private green spaces within the block.
(Courtesy Senator für Bau- und Wohnungswesen)

Figure 41. *Wohnbauten Weser-, Werra-, Inn-Strasse*
The north portion of the park-like interior court.
(Schallenberger and Kraffert, *Berliner Wohnungsbauten*, p. 79)

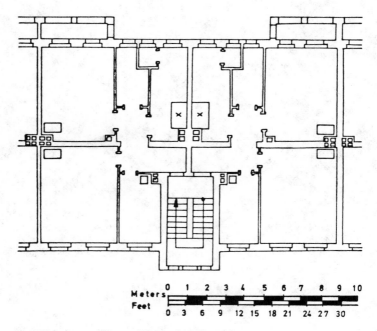

Figure 42. *Wohnbauten Weser-, Werra-, Inn-Strasse*
Characteristic apartment plan of the row-house type. Each apartment is only
two rooms deep, with full exposure to both sides.
(Courtesy Bernd Feuerherd)

Built according to the rowhouse concept, the buildings are one apartment deep and all are arranged with only two units per landing. Sunlight, fresh air and exposure to greenery were amply provided for all residents. The courtyard behind the Innstrasse houses is approximately 62 by 100 meters (170 by 300), with a childrens' playground at the center. This space flows into the other garden-courtyards, also very generous in their proportions and lined with trees and benches. The entire interior of the block becomes a sheltered park space for the residents.

Because of the large dimensions of the site and the strict limitation of building depth, Mebes and Emmerich varied the periphery of the site by opening the center of the eastern side to create the Werraplatz as a forecourt closing the axis of Truseweg. The fact that this street was not cut through as previously planned was a concession by city administrators to the great esthetic benefits of the project to the neighborhood, a rather progressive concession, quite remarkable for this date. The creation of this forecourt, besides providing more units than strictly peripheral development would have, served to articulate what otherwise would have been an overly large interior expanse. The total number of dwellings was increased from 300 to 370 by this court, a substantial increase achieved without sacrificing any of the spatial amenities of the project.

### Strassenbahner Siedlung Müllerstrasse

An interesting variation of the peripheral form in *Siedlung* construction, successfully developed in Berlin in the 1920s, was that of the superblock combining housing with car barns for the streetcar system (today used for buses). One of the finest examples of this type is the transportation workers' housing project and streetcar depot on Müllerstrasse, designed by Jean Krämer[22] (figs. 43, 44).

The Müllerstrasse project in the northern borough of Wedding was built in 1925–27 for the housing cooperative of the transit company, i.e., another paternalistic project. Its location was at the time just beyond the urban fringe of workers' tenements, in an undefined area between the city and the outlying suburb of Tegel. Since the only other depot for streetcars along this major egress route to the north was in Tegel, the need arose for intermediate facilities to provide more efficient service. It was also recognized that a major building project could provide not only acutely needed housing for both drivers and maintenance personnel, but that it could also provide a desirable focal point for continuing urban expansion. The project was thus designed to fulfill three important purposes, which suggests the reason for its strikingly monumental appearance and the bold impact of its visual statement. Since the transit

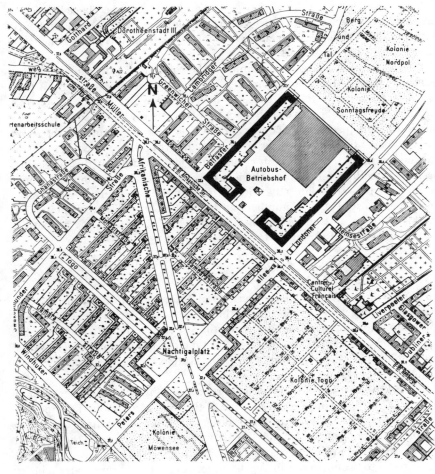

Figure 43.  *Strassenbahner Siedlung Müllerstrasse,* Berlin-Wedding, Jean Krämer, 1925–27
Site plan. A monumental accent in urban development lying toward the suburb
of Tegel, this settlement incorporated peripheral housing with car barns and
landscaped areas.
(Courtesy Senator für Bau- und Wohnungswesen)

Figure 44. *Strassenbahner Siedlung Müllerstrasse*
View of the towers containing offices, community facilities, and water tanks,
seen from inside the complex.
(*40 Jahre Berlinische Bodengesellschaft*, p. 131)

company was responsible for opening large areas of outlying land to development, it was given a design emphasis considered appropriate to its significance.

All four corners of the superblock are set off to provide clear terminal points for the composition. The centers of the long sides, too, are emphasized by being raised a story and being given a distinctive treatment as entrances. Along the wide boulevard of Müllerstrasse the building is taller and provided with shops at ground level. The large entry at the center of this front is treated as a court of honor, flanked by monumental towers containing offices, meeting rooms, and a library in their lower portions and water tanks in the upper. In spite of the enormous dimensions involved, the richly variegated treatment of surfaces and masses precludes any impression of infinite or boring expanses. In fact, the use of wine-colored and purple brick and glazed tile, as well as the expressive use of angled surfaces, pointed shapes, striking shadows, and dynamic rhythms, make this one of the closest approximations to a statement of Expressionism of any building in Berlin.

This settlement provided approximately 380 dwelling units of two-and-one-half or three rooms, with kitchen, bath and loggia. While care was taken to keep walking distances for workers to a minimum, the car barns were separated from the apartments by broad lawns. These ample bands of community green with trees created the effect of gardens rather than industrial spaces and helped convince contemporary observers of the great social concern demonstrated in providing such amenable living conditions for transit workers. A further advantage was the sense of pride, association and loyalty which developed among the company's employees.

## Siedlung Unter den Eichen

The *Siedlung Unter den Eichen*[23] represents a special case, combining the principles of the low-density *Siedlung* with those of the more urban, higher density *Wohnbau*. Unter den Eichen is the name of one segment of the main road leading from the center of Berlin to Potsdam, and is thus a major traffic artery. At the same time, however, its location in Lichterfelde, part of the borough of Steglitz, is distinctly suburban; the character of most of the housing in the area in the twenties was upper middle class, i.e., more expensive, single-family homes with extensive individual gardens, although some multistory, multifamily apartment houses already existed in the area at that time.

Bruno Langkeit, otherwise little known in the literature, was the architect of this project. It was built in 1926–27 for GAGFAH, the building company of the white collar workers' unions, on land belonging to the *Reichsversicherungsanstalt,* a national insurance agency for workers. The settlement was, therefore, another example of cooperation between the unions and their insuring agency, to the end of providing better housing for insured workers. Other than government funding from the house equity tax, limited dividend investing from the major insuring agencies was a prime source of capital for German housing programs of the 1920s.

Since the site proposed for this settlement, although relatively far out from the urban core, was on a major radial thoroughfare, and since a station of the suburban railway *(S-Bahn)* was quite near, there was good reason to consider it an appropriate location for workers' housing, justifying a higher density than normal for such a site. The *Siedlung* was conceived as a frame of three-story apartment buildings surrounding a small garden settlement of semi-detached dwellings (figs. 45–47).

For the sake of a monumental effect, the block along Unter den Eichen was set back at the center to suggest a forecourt and a visual terminus to the cross street perpendicular to Unter den Eichen at this point. The residents, though, could benefit little from such a setback; in fact, the forecourt resulted in the disadvantageous shading of several apartments. The right-angle turns of the two and blocks also reveal somewhat antiquated planning concepts, since they inevitably result in difficult-to-light rooms at the interior corners.

On the other hand, a progressive design feature in this development is the opening of the sunny side, away from the traffic, to lower, more openly spaced semi-detached one-family units. The entire complex thus achieves the quality of contained and oriented space, closed to the outside but open to the inside and to the sun. Quiet, sunny garden spaces are the result, spaces sheltered by the taller buildings. The apartments were intended to be occupied by couples with no more than one child, who would not need individual gardens and could benefit from the greenery and open space of the rest of the development. Although this plan represented a considerable compromise with respect to what then was considered the ideal density for workers' settlements, it seems a reasonable solution for higher-value urban land; in fact, it was one that had been proposed as early as 1910 by Möhring, Eberstadt and Petersen in their prizewinning design for the development of Greater Berlin, referred to earlier.[24]

The Langkeit design for the *Siedlung Unter den Eichen* can thus be seen as a representative solution to the problem of workers' housing in Berlin in the 1920s. Its site planning took into account the developing street and traffic pattern of its environment; it incorporated private gardens and an advantageous orientation to the sun; it created a sense of unity and enclosure within the development; it combined apartment units and single-family homes to achieve a mixed settlement. Finally, it reduced costs by utilizing simple, standardized GAGFAH plans, while focusing attention on amenities of space—the gardens—rather than on form or surface ornament. As is usual for

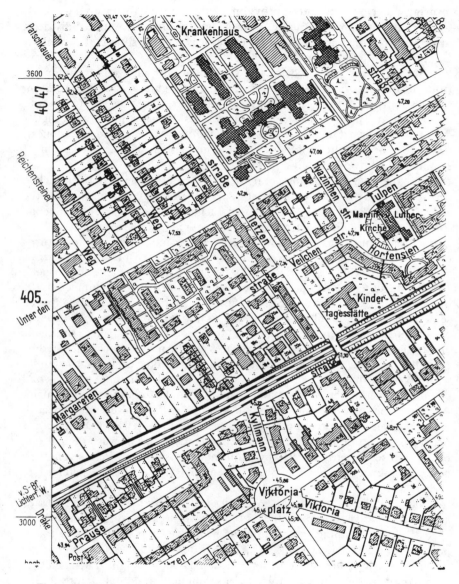

Figure 45. *Siedlung Unter den Eichen,* Berlin-Steglitz, Bruno Langkeit, 1926–27
Site plan. A garden settlement partially surrounded by taller apartment
buildings.
(Courtesy Senator für Bau- und Wohnungswesen)

Figure 46. *Siedlung Unter den Eichen*
"View into the private entrance"
(Schallenberger, *Wohnungsneubau in Berlin*, pp. 24–26)

Figure 47. *Siedlung Unter den Eichen*
Aerial view.
(Schmidt and Ebert, *Wohnungsneubau der Nachkriegszeit*, p. 91)

GAGFAH settlements, while the spaces are well planned, the architecture can easily be overlooked. To achieve a new, healthier way of living one did not require modern form language, and we should also recognize that much progress was made with developments that were intended to blend in with their surroundings.

### Gross-Siedlung Zehlendorf

One of the major and most famous of the *Gross-Siedlungen* in the loose ring of projects built around Berlin in the 1920s is that erected by GEHAG in the southwestern, wooded borough of Zehlendorf.[25] The site is one of sylvan beauty, originally part of a forest in the area, and had been the exclusive domain of villas for the wealthy. In other words, this project was a great innovation for the reformers and a great annoyance for the elite. Breaking the pattern of exclusive enclaves and integrating this suburb in terms of economic class was a revolutionary accomplishment, and the initiative for this bold socialistic thrust of a thousand workers' dwellings came from Martin Wagner, one of the great social champions in Berlin of the twenties.

The *Gross-Siedlung Zehlendorf* was laid out near a rustic restaurant named after Harriet Beecher Stowe's *Uncle Tom's Cabin*. With welcome implications of championing the downtrodden, *Onkel Toms Hütte* came to be the name applied to the station of the subway, when it was extended to this point, and an alternate name for the settlement itself. The first portion was that built south of the present subway line on land at the eastern edge of the forest preserve called *Grünewald*, bounded to the south and east by the small, pleasantly wooded valley called *Fischtalgrund*, which has been made into a park. Since the site itself was wooded, every effort was made to retain the trees, leading to another alternative name: forest settlement *(Waldsiedlung)*. GEHAG's success in obtaining this particular site to provide housing for low-income workers was a triumph in breaking through social barriers. As could be expected, it caused howls of protest from those interested in retaining their privileged status.

It is a tribute to the energy and manipulative talents of Martin Wagner, who had been entrusted in 1926 by GEHAG with the organization and direction of the project, that official approval as well as public financial support from the Housing Welfare Office had been secured for the undertaking before it became public knowledge. Thus, the railing of conservative opponents against this "socialist incursion" were fruitless, and construction of a "satellite town for workers" in the villa suburb was begun.[26]

While Wagner was given the task of overall planning and supervision of the project, the buildings of the settlement were designed primarily by Bruno Taut, with portions by Hugo Häring and Otto Rudolf Salvisberg (figs. 48–56).

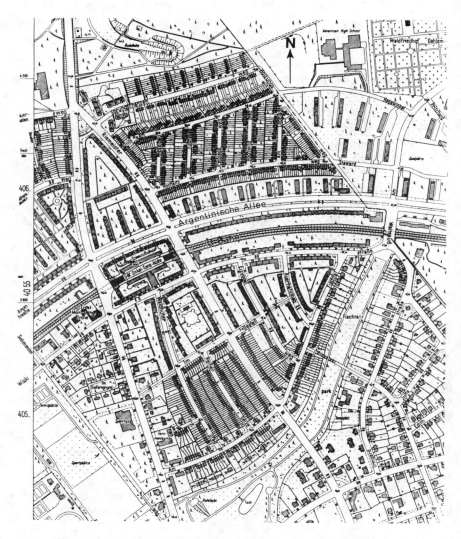

Figure 48. *Gross-Siedlung Zehlendorf,* Zehlendorf, Bruno Taut, Martin Wagner, Hugo
Häring, and O.R. Salvisberg, landscape consulting by Leberecht Migge, 1926–31
Site plan. Division into individual lots reveals which buildings are single-family
row-houses and which contain apartments.
(Courtesy Senator für Bau- und Wohnungswesen)

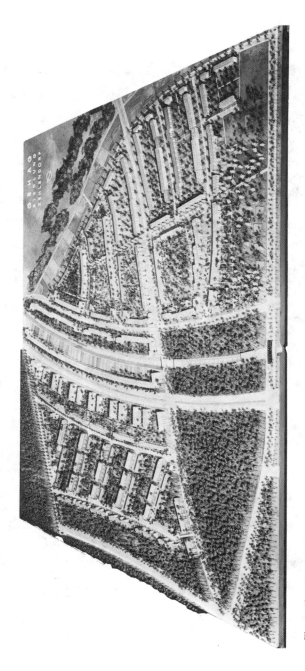

Figure 49. *Gross-Siedlung Zehlendorf*
Model of the site, ca. 1930, prior to the development of the area around the subway station in center foreground. View is toward the east.
(Photo: Arthur Köster. Courtesy Akademie der Künste)

Figure 50. *Gross-Siedlung Zehlendorf*
Semi-private and communal spaces behind Taut's four-family row-houses as they appeared in the 1970s.
(Photo: the author)

Figure 51. *Gross-Siedlung Zehlendorf*
Bruno Taut's row-houses north of Argentinische Allee. View east on Hochsitzweg.
(Photo: Arthur Köster. Courtesy Akademie der Künste)

Figure 52.  *Gross-Siedlung Zehlendorf*
The garden sides of four row-houses by Bruno Taut in a photo ca. 1930. High level of amenity through integration with nature, despite the limited space.
(Photo: Arthur Köster. Courtesy Akademie der Künste)

Figure 53. *Gross-Siedlung Zehlendorf*
A typical living room in one of Taut's two-story apartment buildings, which are essentially four-family row-houses.
(Photo: Arthur Köster. Courtesy Akademie der Künste)

Figure 54. *Gross-Siedlung Zehlendorf*
A typical parents' bedroom in a two-story apartment building by Bruno Taut. Visible at right is part of a tile heating stove.
(Photo: Arthur Köster. Courtesy Akademie der Künste)

Figure 55.  *Gross-Siedlung Zehlendorf*
A typical kitchen in Taut's two-story apartment buildings, with built-ins and stove fired by both coal and gas.
(Photo: Arthur Köster. Courtesy Akademie der Künste)

Figure 56.  *Gross-Siedlung Zehlendorf*
View west on Argentinische Allee in 1933, showing Taut's apartment buildings. Closed construction along the south side and open along the north.
(Photo: Arthur Köster. Courtesy Landesbildstelle, Berlin)

The initial building phase of some 750 units was in 1926–28, and Taut considerably expanded the settlement to the north for GEHAG in three stages in 1929, 1930, and 1931–32. The first phase was composed entirely of two types of building: three-story, single-family rowhouses on the one hand, and two-story, four-family, rowhouse apartments on the other. Generally speaking, in this first phase Taut did all of the four-family units and some of the rowhouses, while Häring and Salvisberg each did about 150 rowhouses in the southern portion of the settlement. Since it was one of the basic aims of GEHAG to achieve the greatest economy by producing a few standard types in large quantities, unit plans were prescribed for the architects. Thus their task was primarily one of site planning, i.e., making the best use of the birch and pine trees and the few existing streets, creating pleasant and interesting spaces in a unified community, and demonstrating by example that adherence to norms and standard types did not have to result in monotony or anonymity.

The principal street of the settlement, which provided direct access to the center of Zehlendorf, some thirty minutes away by foot, was Riemeister Strasse. Its direction, northwest-southeast, determined the alignment of most of the buildings. The minor streets parallel to Riemeister Strasse were made to curve toward the west and were kept free of any through traffic. Also free of traffic was the southern cross-axis, Im Gestell, which, widening and narrowing and offset along its axis, became essentially a pedestrian space. The principal through traffic was on Grunewaldallee (today Argentinische Allee), away from the quiet residential streets. Even today this settlement still serves as a good demonstration of how to minimize the impact of traffic by keeping street dimensions small, alignment inconvenient for anything but access to dwellings, and the visual impression one of discrete community rather than public spaces.

A striking aspect of the entire composition is the intimate and harmonious relationship between the buildings and the spaces with all their trees. There is a strong sense of personal, human-scaled spaces, quiet and peaceful, which is partially due to the collaboration of Leberecht Migge, the fascinating landscape architect who did so much to propagate garden culture for everyone.[27] Buildings were arranged with a concern for a variety of visual effects; movement down each of the curving streets and on the separated network of pedestrian paths is richly rewarding in changing vistas. Longer views down streets are terminated by buildings; there is a conscious enclosure of the planned subway (running in a landscaped cut) and an opening to the gardens, while varied setbacks along the streets create sequences of discrete spaces. Adolf Behne, a constant source of insightful commentary on Berlin in the twenties, has this to say about the success of the Zehlendorf GEHAG settlement:

The Zehlendorf GEHAG buildings form our most successful large settlement. We see in it the prototype of the modern residential city: a happy balance between strict simplicity and cheerful pleasantness. The healthy city-planning solution shows itself immediately in the correctly sensed scale of the streets and in the calculation of their movements. Streets function as spaces, because street and wall have been formed as a unity and no arbitrariness breaks the rows of successive type-houses. The uniformly flat roofs, of course, contribute significantly to the urban picture and emphasize the precision of the spatial qualities. More than in any previous development, all those qualities of the forced or schematic that so easily cling to standardized housing have been avoided, a sign that such qualities need not be a part of standardized building. The tastefully restrained use of color contributes much toward giving the rows of houses cheerfulness and—in spite of all uniformity—personal life.[28]

As indicated above, the GEHAG project in Zehlendorf had been intended by Martin Wagner and his associates to become a satellite town. However, neither the subsequent additions by GEHAG nor the adjacent projects by GAGFAH attained a size or complexity worthy of consideration as a separate town, but the shopping center built up around the subway station (station by Alfred Grenander, 1930; shopping center by Salvisberg, 1931) gave this settlement a greater degree of autonomy than almost any other. While there was no *Stadtkrone* or dominant vertical accent marking the center of the development, Taut did achieve a sense of accent in the taller buildings along each side of Argentinisiche Allee, which repeated the idea of gradation or the containment of a garden settlement as in those we have seen earlier.

Besides containment, though, another idea of the taller buildings along the main street and parallel to the open subway was that, since these units would be less desirable than those surrounding the gardens, they would have to be cheaper and therefore more efficient; hence the three-story apartment buildings. Yet Taut, in this 1930 expansion of the settlement, achieved an interesting variety by treating the south side of the Allee as a continuous enclosing band between subway and street, while opening the north side by placing buildings perpendicular to the street. A lively contrast is established, open versus closed, between the two sides of the boulevard. Opening the north side this way also gave Taut the opportunity to utilize the preferred east-west orientation for dwellings.

Taut's spatial rhythms show other varieties as well: on the north side of the Allee, entrance fronts of alternate buildings face each other across narrower spaces, while the balconied sides face each other across wider spaces of wooded gardens. The preferred side—with balcony and toward the trees— was always the living room side, visually emphasized by its sculptural treatment, opening the dwelling in that direction. In contrast, Taut made the opposite sides—whether facing a street or another building nearby—more planar, reducing the outward orientation of rooms in that direction. Color also was a major element in Taut's composition, with different combinations of red, blue, green, yellow, and white contributing to the distinctiveness of different neighborhoods. Following a period of relative neglect of Taut's esthetic intentions, the late 1970s and early 1980s have seen substantial efforts to recapture and preserve the original effects.

It is perhaps the ultimate irony that the *Siedlung* at Onkel Toms Hütte has been assimilated so well into the wooded suburb of Zehlendorf. Although the personal equity required to purchase the units tended to dictate from the beginning that salaried employees, civil servants, teachers, and other professionals would move in more frequently than the workers for whom the project was ideally intended, there has been, nonetheless, an amazing stability of population in this settlement. Despite the small units and despite increasing standards of comfort during recent decades, this has remained a highly desirable place to live, with a strong sense of community and identity, and a remarkably low turnover rate. How many low-cost housing projects in other countries can make that claim?

Across the street to the southeast one can still see the evidence of the 1928 struggle for people's architectural sympathies: conservative versus progressive, middle-income versus low-income, GAGFAH versus GEHAG, pitched roofs versus flat roofs, bland versus colorful. In what was billed as an exhibition, the *GAGFAH-Siedlung Fischtalgrund* was built in 1928 with detached and semi-detached middle-income homes designed by Alexander Klein, Mebes & Emmerich, Hans Poelzig, Paul Schmitthenner, and Heinrich Tessenow. While the effect then was one of the conservatives thumbing their noses at the social radicals, the consensus today is that their effort was merely undistinguished, while the prize for successful innovation goes to Bruno Taut and his colleagues for the *GEHAG-Siedlung.*

In considering the sequence of housing developments in Berlin, one finds that 1928 was indeed a significant turning point. A shift in emphasis had occurred by that time, partially as a result of economic necessity and partially due to a shift in thinking. Garden settlements of single-family rowhouses with their attached gardens no longer seemed an attainable dream. Focus on solving the housing need of many people led to an emphasis on small dwellings in four-story buildings. While the garden settlement ideal was by no means forgotten, its best features had to be integrated into projects with communal rather than individual benefits. The *Gross-Siedlung,* which until this time had implied primarily a large number of units, came to take on a new meaning—taller buildings, smaller units, and more communal facilities—in the effort to come to grips with the continuing housing crisis.

# 7

# Large-Scale Settlements
# *(Die Gross-Siedlungen)*

## Introduction

A turning point in the development of worker's housing in Berlin came late in 1928, when Martin Wagner and Walter Gropius both published commentaries on the state of housing in that city.[1] They re-evaluated developments up to that time and, each in his own way, made suggestions for the most promising program to satisfy Berlin's housing needs. Both men, among the most influential in the city's architectural circles, recognized that properly designed large-scale settlements *(Gross-Siedlungen)* were the answer to the housing crisis.

This attitude represented a significant change from the architects' earlier advocacy of garden suburbs (*Klein-Siedlungen* or *Stadtrand-Siedlungen),* which had reached their height of popularity in 1926. The low-density, low-rise rowhouses surrounding gardens, once seen as ideal, were considered by 1928 to be only one aspect of the total solution. The most urgent need was for efficient, economical, modern dormitory settlements for large numbers of low-income families. It was imperative that the planning of large settlements be based upon analytical studies of people's basic needs. Just as an ideal minimal dwelling could not be determined simply by shrinking a normal dwelling, so a viable large settlement could not be designed by merely expanding a normal one or producing many units. Basic guidelines for a logical system had to be worked out; the superblock was the essence of the solution selected.

Although various types of project layouts and building arrangements coexisted throughout the twenties, a clear sequence of development in planning thought can be traced through the course of the decade. The starting point was the old style of planning, which called for broad streets flanked by continuous facades of five-story buildings. This continued to be pervasive everywhere one turned in Berlin. What had originally been only peripheral construction had been followed by the systematic filling of the interiors of blocks, as we have seen. While this oppressive density was avoided in new settlements after 1918, much in-fill housing was forced to accept the existing broad streets arranged on a modified grid cut by diagonal or curving avenues. The old-style layout of streets had been continued on urban expansion plans into large areas of undeveloped land, so that a first improvement, given such a street layout, was to build peripherally, but leave the interiors of the blocks open for gardens. This had become the new standard system for settlements.

In terms of building arrangements, much of the experimentation of the twenties consisted in developing variants of this *Randbebauung* theme, generally by opening the periphery at the corners or along one or more of the sides. Offsetting one or more parts of a peripheral band was often done to create a more interesting streetscape or to bring streets and interiors of blocks into more direct communication.

Housing research in Germany during the 1920s generally pursued effective ways of achieving a sense of spaciousness, including an interrelationship between streets and garden spaces. Avoiding dark interior-corner rooms, assuring cross-ventilation, and achieving full exposure to sunshine all became critical issues. This led to the construction of buildings only two rooms deep, an avoidance of building around the corners, and hence to an opening of the ends of blocks. Thus the peripheral arrangement, with buildings on four sides of a block, was transformed to a series of straight rows running in one preferred direction, paralleling the streets on two sides of the block. Since research into the beneficial effects of sunlight emphasized the importance of proper orientation, the favored direction of these rows came to be north-south, yielding both east and west exposure.

Since it also became apparent that the direct fronting of living spaces onto the street was to be avoided if possible because of noise and traffic, the scheme of placing parallel rows of buildings end-on to the street evolved. This was the essence of the superblock, which had the further advantage of reducing the cost of streets. Thus, the development of settlement planning in Berlin in the 1920s may be seen to a large extent as the evolution of variations on the periperal theme, finally resulting in the superblock of parallel rows of buildings evenly crossing large sites: the evolution from pure peripheral building *(reine Randbebauung)* to pure row building *(reine Zeilenbebauung).*

## The Reichs Research Association for Economy in Housing

All of the major large-scale settlements in Berlin in the culminating years of the twenties were *Gross-Siedlungen* of the *Zeilenbau* type, each with its particular variations on the theme. The clearest statement of principles for this important concept was formulated by the Reichs Research Association for

Economy in Housing (*Reichsforschungsgesellschaft für Wirtschaftlichkeit im Bau- und Wohnungswesen,* or RFG for short), which had been formed in 1927 and had its first year of important reports in 1928. Of particular interest is the RFG's national competition for the planning of a demonstration settlement in Berlin in the part of Spandau known as Haselhorst. The competition was held between September and December of 1928, and the most distinguished figures in German architecture took part, either as competitors or as judges.

The panel of ten professionals serving as judges for this competition reads like a *Who's Who* of the German building world, including Otto Bartning, professor and director of the *Bauhochschule* in Weimar; Wilhelm Lübbert, architect and business manager of the RFG; Ernst May, building councilor of the city of Frankfurt; Paul Mebes, professor at the *Technische Hochschule* in Berlin; Dr. Riepert, director of the German Cement Association and also of the RFG; Robert Schmidt, director of the *Siedlungsverband Ruhrkohlenbezirk* in Essen; Fritz Schuhmacher, professor and building director of the city of Hamburg; Eduard Jobst Siedler, professor at the Berlin *Technische Hochschule* and editor of *Die Baugilde;* R. Vorhölzer, building director of the city of Munich; and Martin Wagner, building director of Greater Berlin. Together they judged, and the guidelines they used serve beautifully to summarize the distilled essence—in late 1928—of all German research on revolutionizing workers housing. A paraphrase of these guidelines follows.

To use a peripheral building scheme for small apartments was considered by then to be against advanced planning principles. Parallel rows were preferred, because they assured the best cross-ventilation and an equally advantageous exposure to sunlight for all units. The best arrangement of traffic arteries was considered to be perpendicular to the major axes of the buildings, with footpaths serving as access from the streets to the dwellings. If any buildings at all were to be arranged parallel to traffic streets, they were to be separated from the streets by bands of greenery or by service buildings, such as shops or garages. Residential streets were not to enter abruptly into major traffic arteries (but what kinds of transitional approaches were to be provided was not specified). Existing trees and other distinctive site features were to be taken into account, in order to preserve the landscape character of the setting.

Since the row form was seen as the best and most economical arrangement for apartments, any major breaking of the straight line was considered inappropriate. If rows were laid out on an east-west axis, apartment plans were to be specifically designed for a southern exposure. The two-span arrangement (only two apartments opening from each landing) was considered ideal, but the three-span system was allowed, if provision were made for air circulation through openings in walls perpendicular to each other. Having four apartments opening from one landing was considered unacceptable. The enthusiasm for modern concepts of hygiene was so great that the ventilation of baths and toilets by air shafts alone was also considered unacceptable. Finally, although the use of high-rise buildings was not ruled out on principle, the RFG guidelines stated that the character of the Haselhorst site virtually required low-rise and medium height buildings, i.e., up to four stories.[2]

These guidelines represent the fundamental design philosophy behind all the major *Siedlungen* built in Berlin at the end of the twenties. It is perfectly clear that these rules were not imposed by any individual or any clique or any school. Rather, they were the product of research, exchange of ideas, and building experience of many men over an extended period reaching back to before the war, but especially reflecting progress in the few short years since 1924. The ultimate goal was to establish high quality norms for all working-class housing.

The *Werkbund* housing exhibition in Stuttgart-Weissenhof the year before—while influential in matters of style and advanced in matters of building materials—had dealt primarily with relatively expensive single-family houses (one of them by Walter Gropius and another by Bruno Taut) and had left the major problems of workers' settlements essentially untouched. Even Mies van der Rohe's apartment building at Weissenhof was an expression more of esthetic concern than of economy, although it did incorporate the idea of a flexible dwelling plan through the use of movable partitions.

One of the curious aspects of the RFG competition for Haselhorst is Walter Gropius's participation as a competitor rather than as a judge. As director of the Bauhaus he had been a member of the *Reichsforschungs-gesellschaft* since its inception and had undertaken extensive research projects for it, particularly in his experimental *Siedlung Dessau-Törten*. He was the author or co-author of more technical reports to the RFG than any other individual during 1928, its first full year of operation. Among his interests in architecture while director of the Bauhaus had been building technology and construction methods. As one of the leading figures of the RFG, therefore, Gropius certainly must have been a prime candidate to judge the competition. Yet, after quitting his post at the Bauhaus, he elected to use the RFG contest to other ends and entered the fray with hundreds of others.

The demands of the Haselhorst competition program, it turned out, were so great as to require a new type of engineer/architect/economist team, which had been previously unknown, as the panel of judges recognized. City planning, architectural design, engineering analysis, and economic studies were all required. Attention was to be devoted to an amazing array of considerations, including everything from cost analyses per cubic meter to proposals for the most efficient delivery, storage and emplacement of building materials. Clarification of the means to achieve efficient production was to be included in the design proposal, along with a contractor's competitive bid, all backed up with supporting calculations. Hardly an architect in all of Germany could be expected to meet these ideal and uniquely high expectations.

Walter Gropius (employing multiples of seven for his competition code number 7142128), in an example of the collaboration so important throughout his career, teamed up with the engineer Stephan Fischer to turn out four alternative proposals, each with a more thoroughgoing analysis than that provided in any of the other 213 submissions. There was no competition. The judges commented that the Gropius-Fischer proposals surpassed all others in systematic thoroughness, and were for that reason to be ranked in first place.

The Gropius-Fischer scheme for the site layout was a succession of superblocks with arrow-straight parallel rows brought into exact alignment with the right angle of the two existing major streets (fig. 57).[3] The main difference between the alternatives (A, B, C, and D) proposed by Gropius and Fischer was the height of the rows and the consequent increase of space between them in the taller schemes. The four variations included a range from three-story row houses to twelve-story apartment buildings. Variant D, illustrated here, was the tallest of the four and best represented the concepts Gropius had been advocating, but proved least acceptable in Germany at that time. Ultimately, none of the Gropius-Fischer designs was chosen for the execution at Haselhorst, although a single gallery-access building related to their plans was built there. A superblock layout *was* employed for the site, and the eastern half of the complex was built according to designs by Mebes & Emmerich, while the western half was done by Fred Forbat. For a better, though still only partial, realization of the Gropius-Fischer ideas, one must look to the well-known *Gross-Siedlung Siemensstadt.*

### Gross-Siedlung Siemensstadt

The Berlin *Siedlung* most frequently mentioned in the literature on the history of modern architecture (perhaps because it is the only one in which buildings by Walter Gropius played an important role) is the *Gross-Siedlung Siemensstadt*[4] (figs. 58–63). It was sponsored by the municipality, not by Siemens. Martin Wagner, who is rarely mentioned in connection with this project, was asked to select the architects to design the buildings and to supervise the planning of the settlement. He consulted with Hans Scharoun, who drew up the actual site plans. In *Wasmuths Monatshefte* Werner Hegemann reported on Wagner's obtaining of Hans Scharoun's collaboration in the Berlin housing program, adding that, together, Gropius, Scharoun, Otto Bartning, Hugo Häring, P.R. Henning, and Fred Forbat would be

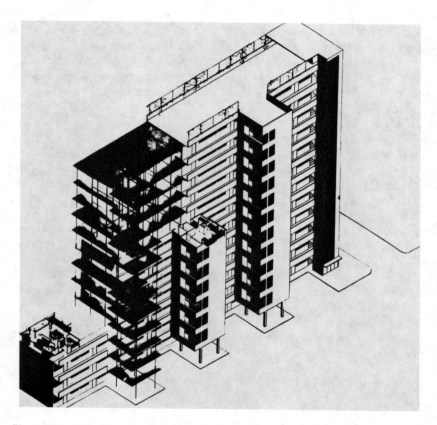

Figure 57. Competition design for the *Reichsforschungs-Siedlung Haselhorst*, Spandau,
Walter Gropius, 1928
Project variant D: high-rise solution.
(Courtesy Bauhaus Archiv)

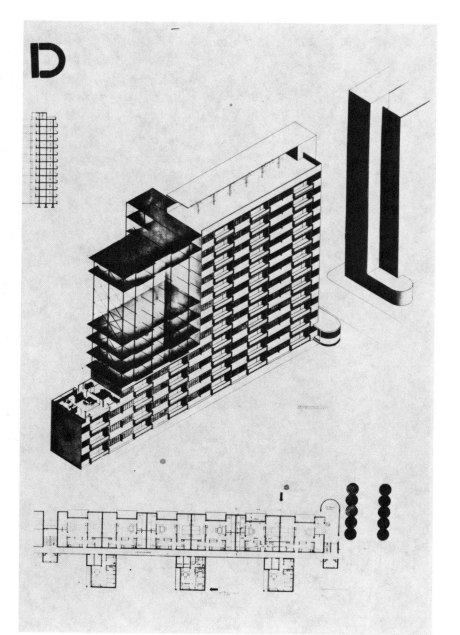

Figure 58. *Gross-Siedlung Siemensstadt*, Spandau and Charlottenberg, Hans Scharoun, Walter Gropius, Hugo Häring, Otto Bartning, Fred Forbat, and P.R. Henning, 1929-31
Site plan identifying contributions of the different architects.
(Courtesy Senator für Bau- und Wohnungswesen)

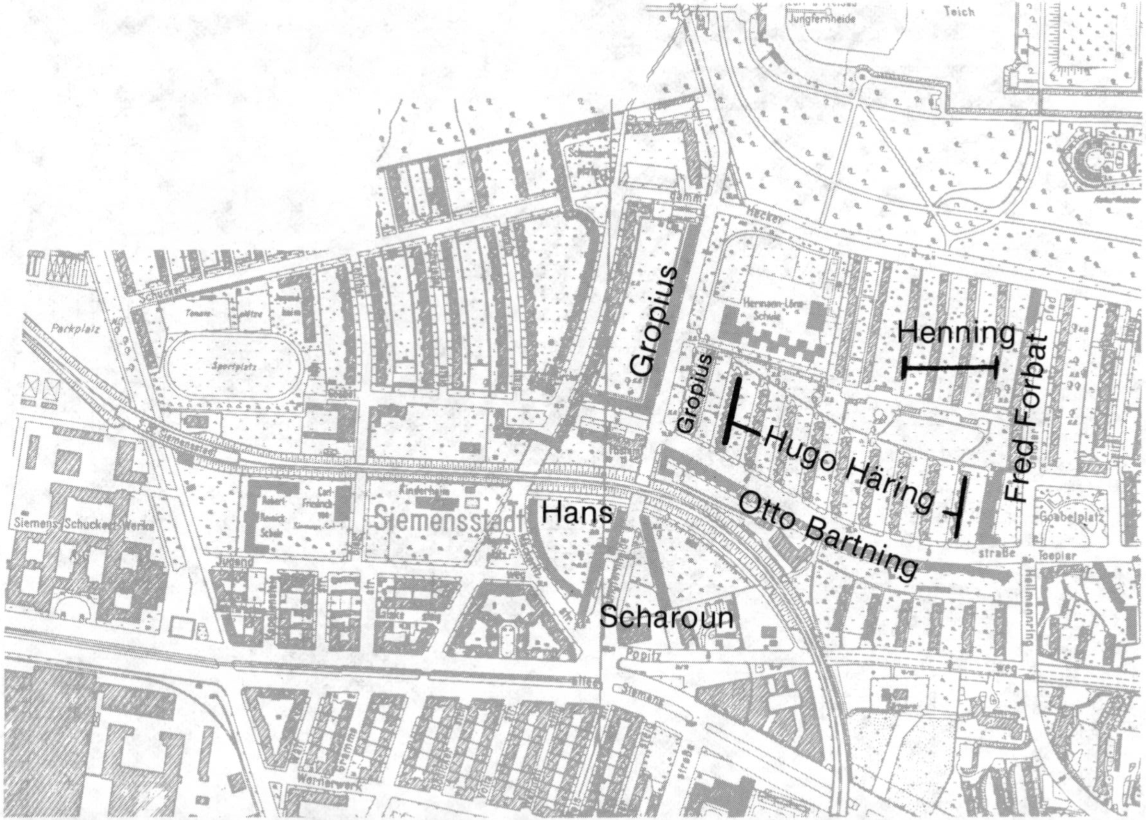

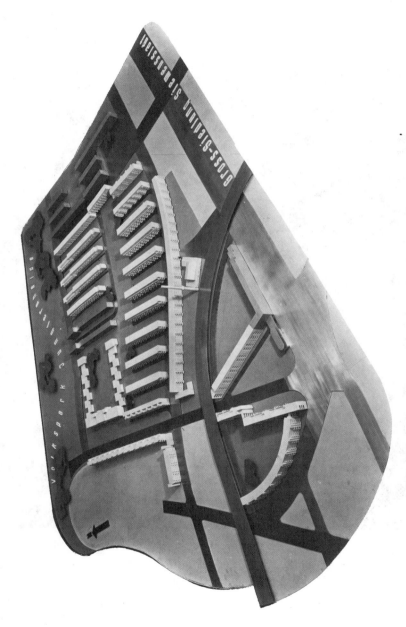

Figure 59. *Gross-Siedlung Siemensstadt*
Model of the site seen from the south, showing the superblock plan.
(Photo: Arthur Köster. Courtesy Akademie der Künste)

Figure 60.  *Gross-Siedlung Siemensstadt*
Interior of Hans Scharoun's own apartment at Siemensstadt.
(Photo: Arthur Köster. Courtesy Akademie der Künste)

Figure 61. *Gross-Siedlung Siemensstadt*, Walter Gropius
Principal block along Jungfernheideweg, with shopping node of the consumers' cooperative.
(Photo: Arthur Köster. Courtesy Akademie der Künste)

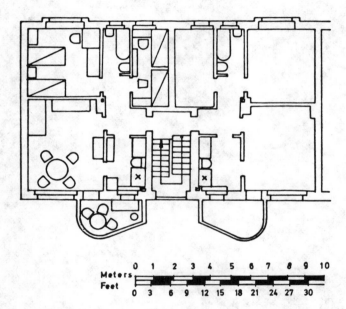

Figure 62.   *Gross-Siedlung Siemensstadt*, Hugo Häring
Floor plan of the 58-square-meter apartments.
(Courtesy Bernd Feuerherd)

Figure 63. *Gross-Siedlung Siemensstadt*, Otto Bartning
Communal laundry facilities. One of the important features intended to facilitate
modern life and to relieve women's drudgery.
(Photo: Arthur Köster. Courtesy Akademie der Künste)

responsible for approximately one-half of the 2,080 units of a supplementary municipal building program, in which city funds were to substitute for those from the house equity tax. Hegemann also referred to the expressionism or fantasy of Scharoun's designs as follows: "The city of Berlin seems to be succeeding in placing even the genius of erratic power, Scharoun, at the service of its practical housing-welfare program."[5]

Of course, by then the association of even expressionist architects with such practical social matters as housing-welfare programs was nothing new. It is one of the most significant aspects of Berlin housing in the twenties that visionary architects, who had expressed themselves in terms of freest fantasy when nothing could be built, turned their energies wholeheartedly to problems of public welfare in housing when the realization of major social goals seemed possible.

As early as 1926 an expression of solidarity among progressive architects—both old and young—had appeared in print as the founding declaration of a group calling itself The Ring:

> By now German architects who follow the newly discovered principles of design have completed their unification, "The Ring"—a self-contained form without a peak—brings together a group of kindred spirits for the purpose of cooperative advancement of their ideal goals. Members of this new organization are: Otto Bartning, W.C. Behrendt, Peter Behrens, Richard Döcker, Walter Gropius, Hugo Häring, Haesler-Celle, Ludwig Hilberseimer, Arthur Korn, Karl Krayl, Hans Luckhardt, Wassili Luckhardt, Ernst May, Erich Mendelsohn, Adolf Meyer, Ludwig Mies van der Rohe, Berhard Pankok, Hans Poelzig, Adolf Rading, Hans Söder, Hans Scharoun, Walter Schilbach, Karl Schneider, Bruno Taut, Max Taut, Heinrich Tessenow, Martin Wagner.[6]

Surely one could hardly imagine a more distinguished list of major figures in early twentieth-century German architecture. Of the six architects chosen to design the buildings at Siemensstadt by their fellow Ring member, Wagner, all but Henning and Forbat were original members of The Ring, and even they were closely associated in sentiment and work with the others. Thus, even though Bruno Taut was not directly involved (in fact, he was occupied at Carl Legien Stadt and in Britz and Zehlendorf, as we shall see), the *Gross-Siedlung Siemensstadt* should be seen as a synthesis of young, progressive architectural thought in Berlin at the end of the decade.

In view of the decidedly middle-class impression Siemensstadt conveys today, we need to remind ourselves that this settlement was specifically planned for lower-income families. Since stringent standards of economy were set, the design achievements are all the more impressive. It was determined that, in order to stretch funds and maximize the number of units, the size of the individual dwellings should be reduced to only 48 square meters. But, since such very small units could easily become unpopular once the period of financial crisis had been weathered, an average area of 54 square meters (about 580 square feet) was set as a reasonable compromise.

The site selected in the northwestern part of the city, at the border of the boroughs of Spandau and Charlottenburg, was in the immediate vicinity of the complex of Siemens factories, to which some fifty to sixty thousand workers commuted each day. Proximity to place of work plus the great amenities of the large adjacent park, the *Jungfernheide,* made this an ideal location for a large settlement. Furthermore, the elevated rapid transit line *(S-Bahn)* had just been extended to this point, providing excellent linkage to other parts of the city.

No streets existed on the site. The development plan incorporated the following fundamental conceptions: the closest possible relationship to the attractive landscape setting, preservation of the stand of old trees, the creation of large interrelated green spaces, the greatest possible exposure to sun, air, and greenery, and the greatest possible economy in street construction. Such considerations—in which one recognizes the research conclusions of the *Reichsforschungsgesellschaft*—clearly mandated a superblock plan, in which most buildings would run north-south and would be accessed from footpaths running perpendicular to the streets.

Significant exceptions, though, were made to this rule. First of all, Otto Bartning's attenuated, curving building band was made to run east-west in order to close the development from the S-Bahn to the south. Secondly, Hans Scharoun's buildings, which lay outside the main development to the south of the tracks, were oriented to create a funnel-shaped forecourt to the *Siedlung* and to accommodate the street pattern west of this court. Scharoun's striking buildings provided a direct visual link to the major traffic artery toward the Siemens plant, Nonnendamm Allee, and acted as an invitation leading the predominantly pedestrian traffic from this street into the settlement and to the park beyond. The third and fourth exceptions to a superblock arrangement were made in the blocks by Gropius at the west and—arranged in a peripheral manner along two streets—and in Forbat's which closed the complex through peripheral building along the street at the east end of the complex.

Gropius was just fresh from his triumph of winning the RFG competition, and Hans Scharoun had just come to Berlin from his critical acclaim at the 1929 housing exhibition in Breslau. This project thus had a great deal of prestige associated with it from the beginning. Scharoun considered the most interesting aspects of it to be the layout of the site, the design of linkages between interior and exterior spaces, the loosening up and enriching of small dwellings, and the challenge of developing a new standard dwelling plan that could win wide support and application in public housing programs.

Notable differences between the goals set for workers' housing early in the decade and at its end are clearly evident at Siemensstadt. No longer is there any mention of the single-family house—however small—on its own piece of tillable soil, which was to bring the urban worker and his family into contact with the earth through subsistence gardening. There are no single-family rowhouses at Siemensstadt: there are no individual gardens; and buildings are taller than the new building code had specified for new land so far out from the central city.

What is the explanation for this apparent transgression against the standards in the one housing project which supposedly so well represents enlightened workers' housing? The answer has two sides, both positive and negative. The negative causes for the deviation from established norms are easy to understand and only serve to make the positive aspects of Siemensstadt more evident. The steadily worsening financial situation in Germany in 1929 made investment capital extremely tight, while the unrelieved, acute housing shortage made it absolutely imperative that something be done to house lower income groups at once. Even greater cost cutting than before now was necessary; the economies of building upward rather than outward seemed unavoidable. Yet—remarkably—height was still limited to a mere four stories.

On the other hand, the positive reason for changing the approach and even modifying the building code at Siemensstadt was an increased understanding of what the real needs of the working class were. The recognition that a need for collective building did not necessarily mean people wanted to live collectively was one part of it. Another part was that, despite abhorrence of the bad conditions in the still predominant rental barracks, removed from all contact with sun and greenery, this did not necessarily mean that all workers wanted to grow their own vegetables. It was important above all else to obtain separate quarters for every family, since there were still hundreds of thousands of people doubling up in cramped quarters. Also important was the need to provide such units without conveying a feeling of mass production, of undue agglomeration. And, finally, the life-giving contact with sunshine, fresh air and greenery was considered a crucial factor. Therefore, in return for all these important amenities—including the sense of a truly park-like setting—special dispensation was granted to allow the buildings to go to four stories. The relationship of the width between to the height of the buildings was a generous ninety-two to forty-two feet, or more than two to one. The delightfully informal landscaping of these community spaces was designed by Leberecht Migge, the landscape architect who had collaborated with Wagner and Bruno Taut at Onkel Toms Hütte.

All the roofs of this *Siedlung* are flat, in keeping with the stylistic preferences of The Ring, although only Scharoun and Gropius made any attempt at utilizing these roofs as terraces for sunbathing (or the drying of wash, although calisthenics is probably what they had in mind). Delight in mathematically pure shapes, in edges cut with surgical precision, in brilliant contrasts between white, seemingly paper-thin spatial envelopes and deep shadows, and in surface rhythms of interesting geometrical shapes pierced in planar surfaces characterizes the work of both Gropius and Scharoun at Siemensstadt, while the others were less purist or less dogmatic, depending on one's point of view. Perhaps the ultimate statement of this consciously anti-traditional, machine-age esthetic was the shiplike, cut-from-steel appearance of the curving forms Scharoun used to enclose his balconies.[7] An interesting contrast to these forms and surface treatments was provided by Hugo Häring in the brownish-yellow brick surfaces with which he topped his buildings and fronted his balconies. This motif was picked up by Forbat, who used it as a horizontal band at the base of his buildings, and also by Henning on his buildings to the north. This combination and contrast of esthetic approaches within one development—coupled with Scharoun's planning scheme—resulted in an ensemble of great variety and interest at Siemensstadt.

One part of the project that was carried out to a lesser extent than originally intended was the grade school and daycare center intended for the main superblock, which one can see on the original plans and models. A high level of communal facilities was nonetheless part of the plan, among them district heating for all units supplied from a central plant, and a modern, fully mechanized laundry and ironing room for all to use. Convenience stores and small restaurant-meeting places were incorporated at different points in the settlement, including a shop of the consumers' cooperative *(Konsumgenos-senschaft Berlin und Umgegend)* linking the two blocks by Gropius.

### Gross-Siedlung Carl Legien Stadt

Bruno Taut, working in collaboration with Franz Hillger, designed and built the *Gross-Siedlung Carl Legien Stadt*[8] at precisely the same time—1929-30— Scharoun, Gropius, Häring, and the others were working on the *Gross-Siedlung Siemensstadt* and at the same time that O.R. Salvisberg and his colleagues were doing the *Gross-Siedlung Reinickendorf*, discussed below. The time had come for large projects and teamwork. At last it was recognized that only through the efficiencies of large-scale building could amenities like efficient modern furnishings and extensive communal facilities—park-like community spaces, kindergartens, nurseries, playgrounds, district heating, central laundries, etc.—be provided for citizens generally. Furthermore, one of the very real advantages to be gained in pursuing large projects was the enormous savings in the red tape which was involved in obtaining building permits and financing.

Carl Legien was named after a prominent leader of the German and international labor union movement and member of the SPD delegation to the Reichstag who had died in 1920. This settlement was the major development undertaken by GEHAG in the year 1929 (along with the expansion of Onkel Toms Hütte) and demonstrates once again the intimate connection between GEHAG, the blue collar unions, and the Social Democratic Party. The intensifying economic pressures of the time are reflected here in the large number of small dwellings and the density of the project. Fully eighty percent of the units are either one-and-one-half or two-room apartments. With a total of 1145 units in four-story buildings on a site about 440 by 210 meters (including streets), the project had a density considerably higher than preferred GEHAG norms. The site was also surrounded by rental barracks and industry: an urban setting as opposed to the suburbs chosen for other *Gross-Siedlungen.*

Bruno Taut concentrated his design efforts on the outdoor, apartment-extending spaces of the settlement, orienting all but a few of his blocks on a northeast-southwest axis, and turning the principal rooms away from the streets, in toward common garden courts, which in turn opened toward the central spine of the settlement, Carmen Sylva Strasse (today Erich Weinert Strasse in East Berlin). This and the fact that all blocks were kept well back from this central street gave the effect, unusual in Germany, of a freely flowing spatial relationship between the various interiors of the blocks (figs. 64–66). Although this is clearly a compromise between the then preferred configuration of parallel rows and the older peripheral building scheme, apartments in interior corners are carefully avoided and a considerable sense of openness is achieved.

A compositional device of Taut's, also seen on his contemporary apartment blocks along Argentinische Allee in Zehlendorf as mentioned earlier, is prominent here. In giving the residents balconies or loggias on the preferred sides, facing green interior court spaces, he made the opposite sides facing the streets relatively closed and planar, thus setting up an expressive contrast of sculptural form. Besides the green courtyards, other communal facilities offered in this workers' settlement included rows of shops, district heating, and a centralized laundry.

### Gross-Siedlung Reinickendorf

Berlin's supplemental building program of 1929, which called for the building of 2,080 new small dwelling units with municipal funds, resulted in two 1000-unit *Siedlungen* in Berlin. As we have seen, the *Gross-Siedlung Siemensstadt* was one of them; the *Gross-Siedlung Reinickendorf*—also known as The White City *(Die weisse Stadt)*—was the other[9] (figs. 67–72). It was designed for the public benefit building company Primus *(Gemeinnützige*

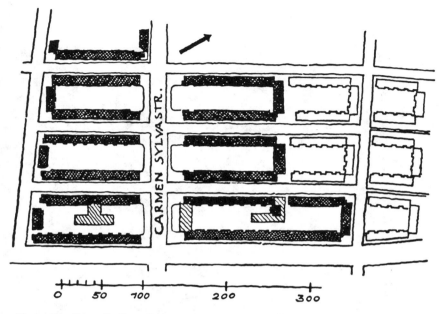

Figure 64. *Gross-Siedlung Carl Legien*, Berlin-Prenzlauer Berg, Bruno Taut and Franz
Hillinger, 1929–30
Site plan.
(Johannes, *Neues Bauen in Berlin*, p. 79)

Figure 65. *Gross-Siedlung Carl Legien*
Blocks on Carmen Sylva Strasse, with gardens opening to the communal space.
(Adler, *Neuzeitliche Miethäuser und Siedlungen*, p. 158)

Figure 66. *Gross-Siedlung Carl Legien*
Two apartment blocks and a shopping node.
(Photo: Arthur Köster. Courtesy Akademie der Künste)

CARNEGIE MELLON UNIVERSITY LIBRARIES
HUNT LIBRARY
Email Renewals: library-renew@cmu.edu

patron's name:COHN, ELIZABETH D

  title:Urban policy under capita
 author:Fainstein, Norman I.
 item id:38482003014129
   due:4/2/2008,23:59

  title:The lost border : the lan
 author:Rose, Brian, 1954-
 item id:38482014041574
   due:4/2/2008,23:59

  title:Staging tourism : bodies
 author:Desmond, Jane.
 item id:38482011609662
   due:4/2/2008,23:59

  title:Berlin's housing revoluti
 author:Wiedenhoeft, Ronald V.
 item id:38482004930729
   due:4/2/2008,23:59


Items subject to recall after 7 days

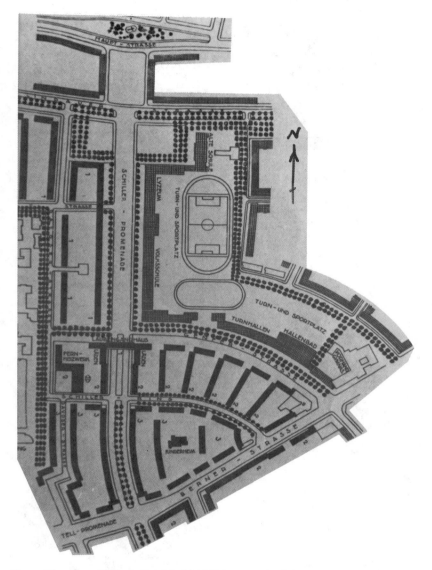

Figure 67. *Gross Siedlung Reinickendorf (Die weisse Stadt),* Berlin-Reinickendorf, Otto
Rudolf Salvisberg, Bruno Ahrends and Wilhelm Büning, 1929–30
Site Plan. Hospital complex off the plan to the left, school and sports complex
to the right, village center of historic Reinickendorf to the north.
(*Die Bauwelt,* XXI [1930], Heft 48)

Figure 68.  *Gross Siedlung Reinickendorf*, O.R. Salvisberg
The bridge across Schillerpromenade seen from the north, with external gallery-access visible.
(*Die Bauwelt*, XXI [1930], Heft 48)

Figure 69. *Gross Siedlung Reinickendorf*, O.R. Salvisberg
The gallery-access or bridge building from the south, with balconies the full width of each unit.
(*Die Bauwelt*, XXI [1930], Heft 48)

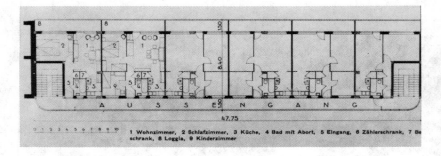

1 Wohnzimmer, 2 Schlafzimmer, 3 Küche, 4 Bad mit Abort, 5 Eingang, 6 Zählerschrank, 7 Be
schrank, 8 Loggia, 9 Kinderzimmer

Figure 70. *Gross Siedlung Reinickendorf,* O.R. Salvisberg
Plan of the gallery-access building, with the gallery or outer corridor on the
north side and the units designed specifically for southern exposure.
(*Die Bauwelt,* XXI [1930], Heft 48)

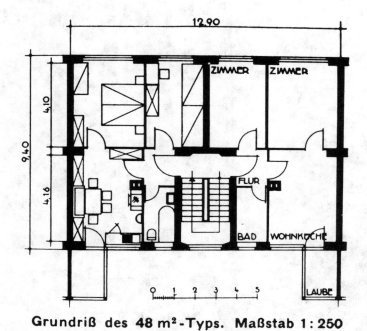

**Grundriß des 48 m²-Typs. Maßstab 1:250**

Figure 71. *Gross Siedlung Reinickendorf,* Ahrends and Büning
Plan of the minimal units of only 48-square-meters, which incorporated kitchen
facilities into the living room, but still included beds for a family of four.
(*Die Bauwelt,* XXI [1930], Heft 48)

Figure 72.  *Gross Siedlung Reinickendorf*
Roof-top view of the complex.
(Adler, *Neuzeitliche Mithäuser und Siedlungen*, p. 175)

*Heimstättengesellschaft Primus m.b.H.),* the stock of which was owned entirely by the city of Berlin. The architects were Otto Rudolf Salvisberg, who had recently completed 150 rowhouses at the GEHAG settlement in Zehlendorf and who was the chief designer here, with Bruno Ahrends and Wilhelm Büning.

The site in the north of Berlin was largely undeveloped. Although an urban expansion plan for the area existed from before the war, some of the streets had not yet been built and therefore could be eliminated in order to accommodate housing in more or less parallel rows on superblocks. The older, tighter radial-and-concentric street pattern had been planned for high-density urban expansion, but, following its incorporation into Greater Berlin in 1920, the area had been down-zoned. While the building of three, four, and even five-story apartment buildings on this land went beyond the intention of the new building code, the necessary dispensation to do so was granted because the plan represented the latest concepts in both efficiency and amenity, i.e., surrounding tall, narrow bands of buildings with broad expanses of greenery, and providing them with a high level of infrastructure. In these respects Reinickendorf was quite similar to Siemensstadt.

In Reinickendorf, three stories were considered optimal. Four stories were considered justified along Schiller Promenade, on esthetic grounds, to balance the four-story school buildings planned on the same street. Five-story blocks were also used for esthetic purposes, to create spatial accents framing the entrance to the project's principal space, Schiller Promenade north of Tell Promenade, and to act as a space container about midway along this wide street space. There, in a dramatic visual statement of the machine-age esthetic, Salvisberg created a hovering horizontal band of gallery-access housing *(Laubenganghaus)* raised on *pilotis* above the flow of traffic. This building was one of the few applications in Berlin of the exterior access system and was also unusual in its use of a reinforced concrete frame construction and in the provision of a large roof-terrace for sunbathing.

The layout and unified esthetic treatment of this settlement made a strong visual statement, expressing clean, efficient modern life and a sense of communal solidarity. Although moderately tall, the housing was surrounded by large expanses of grass and many trees. Coupled with the grouped infrastructure of hospital, school, and sports facilities, the settlement gave the distinct impression of a futuristic satellite community, accounting for its popular designation as *Die weisse Stadt.*

The principal organizing axis for the development is Schiller Promenade, which leads north to the preserved village green of Old Reinickendorf and south toward Berlin. Besides this axis, with a pronounced curve at its beginning, another radial of Berner Strasse has an impact, as do the concentric curves of Schiller Ring and Genfer Strasse, all retained from the old plan. The plaza around which these streets originally would have centered was eliminated in favor of freely flowing traffic and a generous distribution of green spaces throughout. Although certain concessions were made to the existing curving streets, it is clear that there is a characteristic expression of orientation to the sun by having most buildings running north-south. Where exceptions to this were necessary, e.g., in the enclosing terminal blocks at the north ends of courts and especially in Salvisberg's bridge, the units were designed differently to adjust for the fact that the principal rooms faced south. This emphasis on orientation and the physiological and psychological benefits of exposure to the sun is a key characteristic of German housing reform in the late twenties.

The *Gross-Siedlung Reinickendorf* demonstrated yet another significant advance in the technology of housing representative of these major demonstration projects at the end of the decade: a single plant to provide heat and hot water for the whole development. Calculations demonstrating the efficiency of such a system were based upon a thorough investigation, characteristic of the decade's continuous search for more rational technological solutions to the housing problem.

A basic consideration and constraint was the minimal size of the dwelling units. Apartments had already been small, and, as the economy crumbled at the beginning of the thirties, they kept getting smaller. A seemingly impossible challenge confronted reformers and architects alike: with the grip of economic stringency growing ever tighter, how was one to provide the needed quantity and still raise quality to the levels demanded by social responsibility?

Providing heat and hot water from a central source was not motivated by a desire for luxury. The standard Berlin system of individual coal-burning stoves in each dwelling no doubt would have been accepted had it been economical. With the ever shrinking size of dwelling units, however, the proportion of space occupied by the stoves would have become inordinate, and a significant percentage of building volume could be saved by eliminating them. The construction savings gained—plus the costs of the stoves and individual hot-water heaters that were eliminated—more than outweighed the expenses of a centralized system. Standardization and rationalization were fundamental in planning all aspects of the *Gross-Siedlungen*. Every idea was explored as a possible way of improving living conditions, and particular attention was paid to improving the working conditions of housewives. The Germans were fascinated with the time and motion studies of the Taylor system in American industry and applied them to household tasks, and redesigned standard kitchens—such as the famed *Frankfurter Küche*—were one result. In a very real sense, standardization and built-ins became a necessity: old furniture simply no longer would fit.

The development and utilization of norms and standardized parts had remained a constant theme throughout the decade and had been important in all the *Gross-Siedlungen*. The attempt to establish attractive standard dwelling plans of minimal size was constant. Since Reinickendorf was a part of the same supplemental building program as Siemensstadt, the same assortment of unit sizes was required, i.e., thirty percent at 48 square meters, fifty percent at 54 square meters, ten percent at 63 square meters, and ten percent at 70 square meters. Optimizing the depth of the unit (and, hence, also the depth of the building) according to considerations of light, ventilation, heat, and economy, led Salvisberg, Büning and Ahrends to arrive at a standard for the two-room depth of 9.4 meters (circa 30 feet), which is in keeping with the other projects.

At Reinickendorf even the smallest apartments could have four beds, and each unit had a bath and a balcony or glazed loggia. Kitchen facilities, depending on the size of the apartment, varied from wall units in the living room, to curtained alcoves, to entirely separate, small, efficiency kitchens. In all cases the apartments were tightly planned for maximum efficiency, on the assumption that site amenities and the relationship of inside to outside would provide ample living-expansion space beyond the individual dwellings. Apparently a certain amount of conflict arose between the stripped-down, efficient way of life people were expected to lead and the habits and non-standardized furnishings tenants brought with them. Even the light-colored wallpaper supplied to make the rooms seem light and cheery did not at first win the approval of tenants.

The attitude then associated with modernity—cleanliness, brightness, uncluttered efficiency, rationally ordered design, logical simplification down to essentials, and intelligent application of mechanical processes—is implied in the alternative name for the *Gross-Siedlung Reinickendorf*, The White City. Although—with the exception of Salvisberg's reinforced concrete bridge-house across Schiller Promenade—all the houses were of traditional bearing wall masonry construction plastered over, the simple geometry of forms and the white rendering of flat surfaces gave the development a strikingly modern appearance. All floors and stairs were of concrete covered with linoleum. The entire complex of The White City was calculated to express a new way of life, a new social order, a touch of the Fourierist Utopia. It would seem that this was not only a result of methods and materials, but perhaps more directly due to didactic intent. Could people's habits be changed by architecture? Adolf Behne thought not. In explaining the title of his book, *New Living, New Building*, he had earlier said that people first would have to learn new living habits in order to make the new architecture possible. Yet progressive architects, including those at Reinickendorf, were willing to try it the other way around: to attempt to teach people efficient, modern living by putting them into efficient, modern dwellings.

## Extensions to the *Gross-Siedlung Britz*

The years 1930 and 1931, the last to be considered in this study, were catastrophic economically; yet, somehow building activity did continue, although at a greatly reduced rate. Many of the new units in these years were extensions to existing *GEHAG-Siedlungen* in Zehlendorf and Britz, and—while we have already considered some of the former—the latter are worth a closer look.

Of special interest in the Britz extensions is that part south of the horseshoe development, south of Parchimer Allee and west of Fritz Reuter Allee[11] (fig. 20). Here, on what had been open farm land, Taut laid out a plan combining the concepts of gradation, containment, curved and bent axes, rowhouses, and the superblock. The buildings were made to run generally north and south, with all apartments and rowhouses having two-sided exposure, but favoring the east, in the three-story bands of apartments by treating the eastern, convex sides as continuous balconies, and in the rowhouses by attaching individual gardens on the eastern side. Visual containment was achieved not only by the bands of apartments both east and west, but by the unusual terminal apartment blocks *(Kopfbauten)* at the northern ends of the rowhouses (fig. 73). Esthetically, these blocks were treated as visually distinct from, yet clearly related to, the rows, and acted as dominant notes in the composition. By their increase in height and their perpendicular relationship to the rows, they achieved a distinct sense of containment, transforming the negative spaces between rows into designed and contained semi-open court spaces. These court spaces and the houses located on them were accessible only from footpaths, i.e., superblock principles were applied, minimizing the costs of street development and keeping vehicular traffic away from the houses. The spaces between the rows were intimately scaled, designed to be full of greenery, and arranged with various setbacks so as to be visually contained. Taut also worked out a simple but subtle color scheme of maroon, yellow and white, by which he created interest and variation within a clear system.

Other portions of the *Gross-Siedlung Britz* designed by Taut and built in 1930 for GEHAG are those east of Rudower Chaussee (today Buschkrug Allee) and on both sides of Parchimer Allee. Although seemingly lavish in the enormous amount of open land left behind the peripheral buildings and indicative—as are the rowhouses just considered—of GEHAG's continued pursuit of the ideal of workers tilling their own piece of the *Heimat*, these long rows reveal the serious financial pressures GEHAG was experiencing by this time (fig. 74). From an architectural standpoint, the buildings are among the most uninteresting Taut ever built. For the sake of providing the essentials in a workers' housing project, subtleties of planning were dropped in favor of the

Figure 73. Extensions to the *Gross-Siedlung Britz*, Neukölln, Bruno Taut, 1930-31 Aerial photo, 1966. View to the north with the *Hufeisen* visible beyond. Single-family row-houses were still being built in a rearguard action against severe economic pressures in 1930-31. For site plan see fig. 34. (Courtesy Landesbildstelle, Berlin)

Figure 74.  Extensions to the *Gross-Siedlung Briz*

Taut's three-story apartment blocks enclose the gardens and row-houses on the west, north, and east sides. View from the southeast, showing the agricultural land on which the *Gross-Siedlung Briz* was built

starkly simple peripheral layout of such early twenties settlements as the *Siedlung an der Lentze Allee*. Here as there one of the greatest assets was the healthful relationship of the buildings to land, sun, air, and vegetation. But in the building form, Taut simply reused a standard type he had developed for GEHAG, with a planar front toward the street and living spaces with balconies opening toward the gardens. In layout he extended the basic type in a linear fashion to the point of monotony.

### Gross-Siedlung Friedrich Ebert (Friedrich Ebert Stadt)

Named after the first president of the Weimar Republic and incorporating all the progressive concepts of *Siedlung* design of the end of the decade, the *Gross-Siedlung Friedrich Ebert*[12] expresses the political spirit of social reform which is one of the finest aspects of Weimar and one of the most interesting characteristics of Berlin in the 1920s (figs. 75–78). The architects of this settlement were Mebes & Emmerich for the portions between Müller Strasse and Togo Strasse, and Bruno Taut for the portions west of Togo Strasse. The project, built in 1929–31, represents a systematic approach to the problem of the *Gross-Siedlung*.

The designing of this complex had begun in 1928, when the peripheral layout was losing favor to free-standing rows as the best solution to *Siedlung* design. Here free-standing rows were especially appropriate, since peripheral building along the three wide streets (Togo, Afrikanische, and Müller Strasse) would have resulted in excessive noise in most of the apartments. Yet the rows were composed and oriented for reasons of spatial design, rather than following a more dogmatic approach with straight north-south rows, the result of the RFG competition of late 1928. Here the rows were arranged to cut across the axes of the streets in the manner of a superblock, so that most apartments would front on quiet courts, which were given a greater sense of containment by the offset blocks at the ends of rows. Along Müller Strasse, the most heavily traveled street (and opposite from Jean Krämer's car barns and streetcar settlement considered earlier), the buildings are five stories tall. On the opposite, west side, toward the large, adjacent Rehberge Park, the height was decreased to three stories, with four stories the standard throughout the rest of the settlement. Anticipating the potential disadvantage of a superblock system—that the walking distances to streets could become excessive—the site plan was altered by penetrating the settlement with two culs-de-sac entering from the northwest.

Despite the planarity and standardization, a surprising variety and interrelationship of spaces was achieved in the *Friedrich Ebert Siedlung*. Garden spaces in the eastern triangle were shielded from the busy Müller Strasse by a one-story band of shops. Within the settlement monotony was

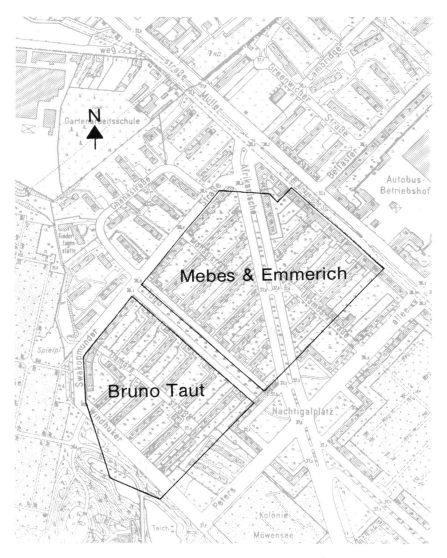

Figure 75. *Gross-Siedlung Friedrich Ebert,* Berlin-Wedding, Mebes & Emmerich, and
Bruno Taut, 1929–31
Site plan with portions east of Togo Strasse by Mebes & Emmerich and
portions west of it by Bruno Taut.
(Courtesy Senator für Bau- und Wohnungswesen)

Figure 76.  *Gross-Siedlung Friedrich Ebert*
        Mebes & Emmerich's buildings east of Togo Strasse.
        (*Wasmuth's Monatshefte*, XVI [1932], pp. 429–35)

Figure 77. *Gross-Siedlung Friedrich Ebert*
Apartments and shops on Müllerstrasse
(Photo: the author)

Figure 78. *Gross-Siedlung Friedrich Ebert*
Garden court and entrance detail in a block by Bruno Taut.
(Photo: the author)

avoided, first, by offsetting the axes of rows and, second, through the calculated use of offset terminus blocks *(Kopfbauten)* at the ends of the rows. These, in the Mebes & Emmerich portion, were brown as opposed to the light gray and white of the rows, and especially along Afrikanische Strasse, which is higher than the surrounding grade, these terminus blocks were raised half a story and offset from the principal blocks. Taut also used *Kopfbauten,* which he raised by adding a full story, as accents and as closing elements for the gardens. He further enhanced the feeling of enclosure by bridging the internal access street where it entered from the north.

Throughout the settlement, access to the apartments was provided from the north, so that stairwells, along with kitchens and baths, were kept to this side of the buildings, while the south side was reserved for balconies (in Taut's buildings) or glazed loggias (in the Mebes & Emmerich blocks) and for the living rooms and main bedrooms. The general effect of machined, industrial shapes was achieved entirely with traditional building methods: foundations were poured concrete, while all walls were bearing-wall masonry covered with painted stucco treated to resist penetration by dirt and water. In providing modern facilities, including district heating and central laundries, the *Friedrich Ebert Siedlung* met all the standards of modern *Gross-Siedlungen.* Along with its rational efficiency and somewhat assertive modern form-language, it provided a good sense of openness despite a relatively high density, and a sense of contained, semi-private spaces despite the openness.

### Die Feuer- und Rauchlose Siedlung

The clarity and precision of Mebes & Emmerich's buildings in Steglitz, built for GEHAG, express the direction taken in advanced *Siedlung* design in Berlin by 1930: pure row building on a superblock, with stripped-down geometric forms as an expression of lightness, clarity and efficiency. The perceived challenge was to put modern technology to work in the service of low-cost housing, and the esthetic intent was to convey the message that it was indeed happening. Naming this settlement Fireless and Smokeless[13] was another way of stressing modern technology's achievement in eliminating both fire and smoke from housing, a benefit still sorely lacking in most major cities of the world more than half a century later. This was accomplished by supplying all kitchens with electric stoves and providing district heating from a municipal heating plant removed from the settlement.

Professional debate concerning the relative merits and demerits of superblocks with straight, parallel rows was quite active around 1930. While it was recognized that transforming any scheme into dogma was no substitute for creative design in housing, it was concluded that parallel rows uniformly crossing a large site had many advantages to offer. In fact, for this site the use of the system had been predetermined by the building councilor for the borough of Steglitz, Fritz Freymüller, in his master plan.

The Fireless and Smokeless consisted of two parts, one part with rows perpendicular to Mariendorfer Strasse (today Steglitzer Damm) designed by Mebes & Emmerich, while the other part, on both sides of Munsterdamm, was by Heinrich Straumer (figs. 79–82). By varying the setbacks, staggering buildings forward as the street curves west, and turning some of the buildings ninety degrees along Munsterdamm, Straumer achieved a lively interplay of spaces between rectilinear buildings and curving street, creating a changing vista of building ends as one moved south along the street. Concerning his portion, Mebes wrote that it was precisely the contrast with the endlessly repetitive, continuous facades of normal Berlin streets that made the system of open rows so charming, so lively, so full of change. Instead of constant closure along the sidewalks, there was the alternation of buildings and gardens. Instead of continuous hard surfaces, there was space and greenery to be experienced from the street. Four out of the seven gardens so created between blocks were closed at their northern ends by low cross-buildings which contained a common laundry for each pair of apartment blocks.

The machine-made appearance of the buildings supposedly resulted from the consistent application of industrial techniques wherever possible, but was undoubtedly also a stylistic choice. Technical determinism was also used to justify the parallel rows as encouraging a high degree of rationalization in construction. For efficient methods and materials handling Mebes gave special credit to Otto Müller, director of the construction firm of Philipp Holzmann A.G., which carried out the project. Finally, rationalization and standardization were applied not only for the sake of economy and efficiency but for the ultimate goal of cheap but pleasant dwellings which would be practical to use and would provide a healthy contact with nature. One senses the goal of creating a new lifestyle through a new and different environment, a goal seemingly attained in such settlements as the *Feuer- und Rauchlose Siedlung.*

### Siedlung Heimat

Hans Hertlein, whose industrial buildings for the Siemens electrical concern drew international praise throughout the twenties and whose earlier Siemens housing had been so picturesque, designed a large settlement of company housing near the Siemens factories at the end of the decade[14] (figs. 83, 84). His earlier *Siedlung* just to the north was expanded at the same time by the addition of three-story apartment buildings, but his major contribution to housing was this large complex just west of the *Gross-Siedlung Siemensstadt,* of the same size (1,000 units) and built at the same time. Since his was designed

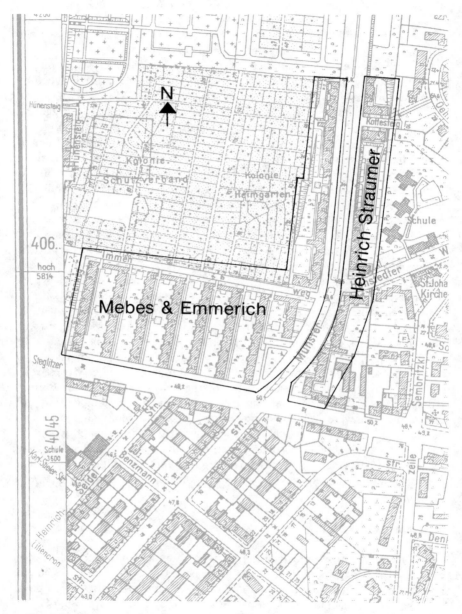

Figure 79. *Feuer- und Rauchlose Siedlung,* Berlin-Steglitz, Mebes & Emmerich, and
Heinrich Straumer, 1930–31
Site plan, showing the advantages of the superblock concept and the
relationship to the open, green area of the allotment gardens to the north.
(Courtesy Senator für Bau- und Wohnungswesen)

Figure 80.  *Feuer- und Rauchlose Siedlung*
Aerial view shortly after construction.
(Heilig, *Stadt- und Landbaukunde*, p. 76)

Figure 81. *Feuer- und Rauchlose Siedlung*
Among the advantages of the superblock can be the exposure of all units on both sides to quiet, green areas. A characteristic space between buildings by Mebes & Emmerich as seen in the 1970s. (Photo: the author)

Figure 82.  *Feuer- und Rauchlose Siedlung*

Another advantage of the superblock is the relief of the tedium of continuous walls around the perimeters of blocks. Instead, as here, the landscaped garden spaces can also enliven the street. Photo 1970s. (Photo: the author)

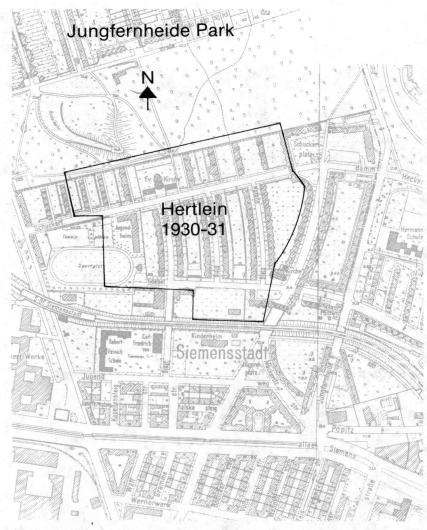

Figure 83. *Siedlung Heimat,* Spandau, Hans Hertlein, 1930–31
Site plan. While not a superblock plan, the site layout takes great advantage of
relationships between the units and generous open green spaces. The interiors of
the blocks are fenced off, creating semi-private spaces.
(Courtesy Senator für Bau- und Wohnungswesen)

Figure 84. *Siedlung Heimat*
Curving street axis toward the Protestant Church. Photo 1970s
(Photo: the author)

as a single entity, it easily surpassed its more famous neighbor in terms of standardization on a large scale.

Hertlein's buildings were all three-story apartment blocks running in a generally north-south direction. The principal roads on the site ran east and west, fanning out noticeably toward the east. The underlying plan, based on these axes, was to have subsidiary streets and building bands connecting the two roads and meeting them perpendicularly, hence the slight curvature to the east. At four entrances to the settlement buildings were bridges over the streets, creating arched entrances and a strong sense of containment as well as a visual and psychological separation from the settlement by the Ring architects to the east. The name *Heimat,* with all its connotations of conservatism and a high regard for tradition, suggests that the building of a wall against the east may have been intended to have distinctly political implications.

In any case, it is clear that Hertlein avoided the application of the superblock system on a site and under conditions that almost required it. Instead, he returned to a modified form of the old peripheral layout *(Randbebauung),* somewhat related to Taut's application at Carl Legien Stadt, but under entirely different circumstances and with an entirely different visual effect, strikingly traditional in Hertlein's case. Here, too, the garden spaces, instead of flowing into the street spaces and creating linkages throughout the settlement, are closed off by tall garden walls at the north and south ends. Picturesque effects abound: the curving street facades, the arched entryways, the plaza spaces created at the northeast and southeast corners, and the use of the tower of the Protestant church to terminate the vista along the central north-south axis. The added touch of sgraffito used on some of the balconies—also employed in Hertlein's contemporary additions to the *Siedlung Siemensstadt*—was a nod toward South German tradition and an apparent attempt to soften the effects of mass production and standardization. Furthermore, the flat roof—by 1929 associated not only with concepts of rational modernity but also with an impatience to change society—was assiduously avoided by Hertlein. The flat versus pitched roof controversy had become so much an expression of political conviction that Hertlein's roofs—certainly no less rational than those of the *Gross-Siedlung Siemensstadt*—were seen as expressing a sociopolitical stance.

Werner Hegemann—who, it will be remembered, favored an architecture of straightforward simplicity—made the observation that Hertlein's project was built to satisfy the age-old needs of living and would retain its value independent of the demands of fashion.[15] Such objectivity, however, rarely sets the tone for the critical judgment of time. In retrospect, it might instead appear that Hertlein's unwillingness to apply the latest principles of planning and his desire to avoid modern form language was an early expression of the reactionary conservatism characteristic of National Socialist architecture of the 1930s. While it is true that the kind of conservatism evident here had been present in Berlin throughout the twenties, it is also true that the primary distinction between the progressive work of the Ring architects and the more traditional appearance of Hertlein's development had to do with patronage, as observed earlier. Whereas the *Gross-Siedlung Siemensstadt* was commissioned essentially by the municipality acting in accord with the housing program of the Social Democrats, their *Stadtbaurat* Martin Wagner, and the labor unions, Heimat was company housing built as a paternal endeavor. Yet despite this distinction, and despite the charm and value apparent in Hertlein's design, in retrospect it seems to demonstrate the beginning of a regression from the great advances that had been made in workers' housing up to that time.

### Strassenbahner Siedlung Knobelsdorff Strasse

Jean Krämer, the architect of the highly successful and much-praised transportation workers' housing and streetcar yards on Müllerstrasse in Berlin-Wedding, was later called upon to design similar projects for the Berlin transit company, one in Charlottenburg and one in Britz.[16,17] As in Wedding, both of these projects combined the streetcar yards with company housing built by the paternalistic *Gemeinnützige Heimstätten-Baugesellschaft der Berliner Strassenbahn.* The project in Charlottenburg, fronting on Königin Elizabeth Strasse, is truly monumental in a new way, distinctly fascistic in its overbearing classicism (fig. 85). It was made to look even larger than it actually was by being combined visually in one unified design with a separate project mirroring it on the other side of the grand central axis of Knobelsdorff Strasse. The portions along this street exude bombast, including flanking eight-story towers, and responsibility for the design belongs to Krämer, although O.R. Salvisberg assisted in designing some portion of the housing. Later expansion of the settlement to include more housing was also designed by Krämer.

The concept developed here was neither garden settlement nor dormitory community in a quiet, open environment. Rather, the idea was to reverse the trend of industrial societies toward the separation of dwelling and place of work. The Taylor system of time and motion studies, already mentioned, played a significant role in transforming industry in the 1920s and came to be considered an important expression of modern life: a method of analysis leading to desired efficiency. By extension, it could be applied off the job as well as on, leading to the idea that if it was important for a man not to lose a minute of productive work, it was just as important that he not lose hours of productive life imprisoned in the transportation system to and from his place

Figure 85.  *Strassenbahner Siedlung Knobelsdorff Strasse,* Charlottenberg, Jean Krämer and O.R. Salvisberg, 1930
Monumental formalism signals the beginning of a period of reaction.
Photo 1960s.
(Photo: the author)

of work. While it is clear today, decades later, that this fundamental paradox of modern life is unlikely to be resolved, it is interesting to see the transit company in Berlin leading the way in attacking the problem of commuting, as least for its own employees.

Krämer was credited with being one of the first architects to reunify dwellings with places of work. He was apparently convinced that a significant reduction in commuting was imperative if chaos was to be avoided on the streets of the metropolis. Yet, admirable as the basic conception was, distinctly retrogressive features reduce one's enthusiasm for the *Strassenbahner Siedlung* in Charlottenburg. The most obvious of these is the overbearing employer image inherent in a complex of this type and size. Although the need for the peripheral arrangement can be understood in this case, where housing was combined with car barns, one wonders why it had to be so heavy-handed and so unmitigated by vegetation or other spatial amenities. The resulting large container, here pushed to five stories, became a ponderous monument . . . to what? To the power of authority? Symbolic form seems to have relegated quality of life to a minor role, and generally accepted values of advanced housing played a secondary role to tedious posturing. Josef Thorak's sculptural family of hero types in stone flanking the symbolic entrance to this settlement as a Monument to Labor completes the heavy rhetorical imagery.

To see the reappearance of monumentality and classic formalism expressed in the facade of five-story peripheral housing on large sites is to experience a rebirth of old rental barracks ideas. Formal expression at the expense of spatial amenities is the antithesis of advanced workers' housing. One need look no further: the *Strassenbahner Siedlung Knobelsdorff Strasse* symbolizes the end of 1920s' liberalism and the beginning of a period in which significant advances that had been made were largely denied and negated. A period of regression into architectural conservatism and social reaction had begun. The two phenomena are clearly linked.

## The Question of Tall Housing

Before ending our consideration of the large-scale settlements, we should devote some attention to the idea that tall buildings might be the most suitable form of workers' housing. Although high-rise construction did not play any role in housing in Germany during the twenties, its increasing role after 1950 and vigorous challenges to its validity since the late 1960s suggest that thoughtful consideration should be given to its early development in the twenties.

We know that high-rise building was an essential feature of Walter Gropius's plans to improve urban housing and the urban landscape. As late as

1955 in *Scope of Total Architecture* Gropius employed the same set of diagrams to espouse the purported advantages of high-rise housing which he had first brought forth in the twenties. The advantages are as follows: 1) Assuming the same sized plot and the same angle of incident light (defined as the angle above the horizon of a line connecting the top of one building with the base of its neighbor), the number of beds that can be accommodated increases with increasing numbers of stories. 2) Assuming the same angle of incident light and the same number of beds accommodated, the amount of open land increases with increasing numbers of stories. 3) Assuming the same sized plot and the same number of beds accommodated, the angle of incident light decreases with increasing numbers of stories, thus achieving more advantageous lighting and a great increase in spaciousness.[18]

The twenties, as we know, were not ready to accept high-rise dwellings. Not only were such buildings unacceptable under existing building codes, their suitability as housing was seriously questioned by many progressive architects, who perhaps sensed that site density or numbers of beds would not remain the same in high-rise settlements. Furthermore, while exposure to sun, greenery and space was universally considered important and necessary, this did not mean that the benefit to be gained would continue to increase proportionately as the distance between buildings increased. In the RFG competition, the Gropius-Fischer variant D (which surely must have been Gropius's own favorite) was rejected by the judges of the *Reichsforschungsgesellschaft* on the grounds that it was not appropriate for local conditions.[19]

High-rise dwellings as a solution to the problem of workers' housing did not play a major role even in theoretical considerations in Berlin during the twenties. Interestingly, though, at the Bauhaus, as an aspect of the pursuit of technological futurism in research and development, the idea seems to have been expressed earlier and pursued further by Marcel Breuer than by Gropius. Its first appearance at the Bauhaus is surprisingly early, in 1924, in the form of a model by Breuer (fig. 86).

The conception, development and technology of the tall building in Germany is a theme requiring consideration in a separate study. That Marcel Breuer played an important role is quite clear. For the competition to develop a new dwelling form *("Das Bauwelt-Haus"),* conducted by the periodical *Bauwelt* in 1924, Breuer had submitted a six-story gallery house model, which served as the prototype for his later high-rise slab designs (fig. 87). Also working at the Bauhaus in the same period, Georg Muche had prepared a design for a fifteen-story apartment building conceived in terms of steel and reinforced concrete prefabricated panels (fig. 88). Both designs were amazingly forward-looking for their time.[20] Unfortunately, it seems impossible to determine today how many of the 213 other entrants in the *Reichsforschungsgesellschaft* competition of 1928 might have proposed high-

Figure 86. Drawing for a high-rise dwelling, Marcel Breuer, 1924
(Courtesy Bauhaus Archiv)

Figure 87. Competition design for the *Reichsforschungs Siedlung*, Spandau-Haselhorst, Marcel Breuer, 1928
(Courtesy Bauhaus Archiv)

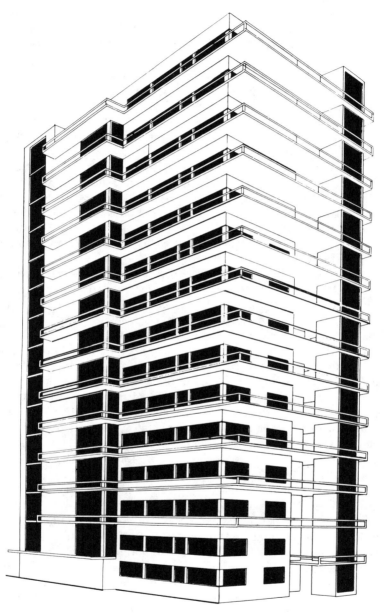

Figure 88.   Drawing for a high-rise dwelling, Georg Muche, 1924
(Courtesy Bauhaus Archiv)

rise solutions for the Hasselhorst site. Breuer, who was among those eliminated from consideration, salvaged his work (prepared with the assistance of Gustav Hasenpflug) for publication in an article on high-rise buildings in *Die Form*.[21] His design for Haselhorst must have been the tallest of the tall.

Where Gropius had planned six rows of twelve-story buildings, Breuer had three long rows eighteen stories tall, giving a striking impression of overwhelming scale and awesome regularity. As much as these high-rise slabs differed from the housing standards of the RFG at the time, one recognizes that the thinness of the slabs—two rooms only—as well as the east-west orientation of all apartments and the spacious green areas surrounding the buildings were precisely in agreement with programmatic aspects of progressive workers' housing settlements. His was merely an extrapolation of the same principles from three- and four-story walk-ups to tall elevator buildings. Furthermore, Breuer combined his tall slabs with the popular idea of garden settlements: single-family, two-story rowhouses with attached gardens. He interposed the rowhouses between his rows of tall slabs, achieving a startling juxtaposition of the two extremes of housing form.

Breuer justified this bipolar answer to contemporary housing needs as most timely. On the one hand, the private dwelling, intimately connected with nature, had the mother working at home and the family spending its spare time working in the garden, keeping healthy and saving money by growing vegetables. On the other hand was the apartment in a high-rise building. Here household work was to be reduced to a minimum by a broad range of well organized communal facilities, freeing the woman for a more independent life and the possibility of working outside the home. Community sports facilities were to provide a substitute for working in a garden. Breuer was thus taking care of the needs of two paradigms of modern life with his two types of dwelling, but strongly emphasizing the second in keeping with his perception of the significantly changing role of women in society. Women's liberation was an important issue at the Bauhaus and, to a lesser extent, in German society generally in the 1920s.

Ludwig Hilberseimer, city planning specialist in the Bauhaus circle, must also be mentioned in connection with high-rise workers' housing. He was active as an architect in Berlin and had worked in close association with Mies van der Rohe as a planning consultant since 1919. Hilberseimer's primary contribution during the 1920s was theoretical, both in design projects and in his commentary on works by others. His books made an important contribution to the modern movement in the twenties. In design he developed projects for rowhouses and apartment houses, as well as a highly systematized scheme for a high-rise urban core, which, however, lies outside the scope of the present study. His work in the period here under consideration culminated in

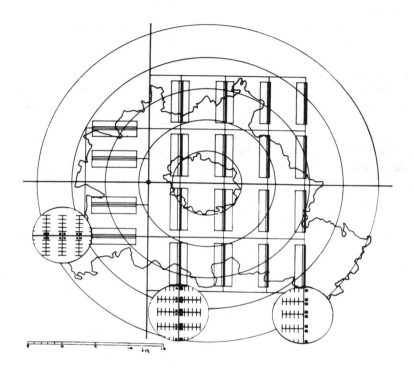

Figure 89.  Project designed for a mixed settlement of row-houses and high-rise slabs,
Ludwig Hilberseimer.
(Courtesy Bauhaus Archiv)

a mixed settlement *(Mischsiedlung)* consisting of high and low-rise buildings, apartment houses as well as single-family dwellings (fig. 89). This remained for Hilberseimer the most valid product of his studies.

The theme of the 1931 building exhibition in Berlin was the Dwelling of Our Time, and it was under this title that Hilberseimer published his conception of the mixed settlement (along with other designers' concepts shown with his at the exhibition).[22] After reporting on Gropius's standard presentation of ten-story parallel slabs, Hilberseimer showed his scheme for a mixed settlement. A landscape extending to the horizon was divided into a rectangular grid pattern of major and minor roads, with seven of every eight sections devoted to one-story rowhouses with gardens. One section in every eight was treated as a superblock crossed by ten-story gallery access buildings. The combination was similar to Breuer's for Haselhorst. Hilberseimer, however, reversed Breuer's proportions of people living in rowhouses to those inhabiting small efficiency units in high-rise slabs.

# 8

# Conclusion and Epilogue

The *Siedlung* concept in Germany in the 1920s emphasized the combination of a decent dwelling in a healthy, natural environment with the advantages of city living: education, transportation, and opportunity for work. Unfortunately, a severe housing shortage remained throughout the twenties in all major urban centers, but especially in Berlin. Despite the great surge of new building activity, which reached a peak in 1927, the number of families without adequate housing steadily increased in Berlin because of the constant influx of new city dwellers.

Berlin was a magnet, not only as the cultural, commercial and political capital of Germany, but also as—along with Paris—one of the most dynamic centers in all of Europe at the time. Approximately 35,000 families moved into Berlin each year of the 1920s, and over 40,000 marriages were registered annually. Yet in 1927 the census showed that over 113,000 families in Berlin were still living as subtenants because no separate housing was available for them.[1]

In retrospect, it seems most impressive that, at a time when there was such dire need for any kind of housing, there should have been such concern for creating high-quality housing for the poor. Fundamental to all the research on and development of workers' housing was this humanitarian attitude, despite great adversity. The pressing need made it apparent why this one segment of the economy could not be left to the free market.

The justification for public service building corporations, such as GEHAG, was that the market system of supply and demand had ceased to function for low-cost housing. Furthermore, unlike other competitive, marketable commodities, housing had not responded to attempts at regeneration.[2] The only solution found was a system of government support and supervision for a large-scale, non-profit public housing program. Workers' housing had to become a public enterprise. The transformation from a speculative business operated solely for maximizing immediate returns to a long-term public investment was crucial. Housing construction came to be considered an essential public service and was therefore subjected to public scrutiny, planning and control.

The source of funds for the impressive amount of public support for housing construction in Prussia was the House Rent Tax or House Equity Tax *(Hauszinssteuer)*, levied on all buildings built before the war. This tax had been proposed as early as 1916 by Martin Wagner as a device for alleviating the housing shortage already then existing. When finally passed into law in the spring of 1924, this special tax on the rents or values of pre-war buildings was intended to tax unearned profit increments for the sake of the general welfare. Since the devastating inflation had erased the value of all mortgages, it had effectively presented house owners a large part of the value of their property for nothing. The income from this tax was used to finance the government-sponsored housing construction program, primarily through forty percent second mortgages at a mere one or two percent interest.[3]

The funds collected from the house rent tax soon surpassed personal income tax in total volume. However, as chancellor of the Reich in 1925, Hans Luther was instrumental in channeling more than fifty percent of these funds away from housing construction into general revenues. This was the same man, who—as secretary general of the German Association of Municipalities *(Deutscher Städtetag)*—had vigorously opposed the tax when Martin Wagner had originally proposed it in 1916. The ultimate fate of the public housing program was sealed in 1931 when all of these funds were diverted to other purposes.

The solution to the problems of housing shortage and housing quality had been sought in a controlled, non-profit system of housing construction. Between the years of 1924 and 1930 a total of 135,000 dwelling units were built in Berlin using public funds. The vast majority of these were small units. Considering an average occupancy of three and one-half people per unit, new quarters for a population of over 470,000 persons had been provided in Berlin during that seven-year period.[4] The great advantage of government support of a building program of this scale was the unusual opportunity it provided to have direct control exercised over the quality of the units constructed. The great weakness in the program was the government's failure to exercise sufficient control and its failure to utilize the available funds to assure steady production. In 1928 Martin Wagner pointed out the paradox of a constant source of income from the house rent tax and the wildly fluctuating rate of production in housing construction.[5] In 1926 the number of dwelling units completed per month had fluctuated between 677 and 2,681; in 1927 between 1,059 and 2,367. In 1928 the range was between a low of 539 and a high of 2,201 units. As a result, not only were insufficient units produced, but 20,000 building trades workers in Berlin and vicinity had to draw unemployment support during low periods.

In spite of all the achievements, there were still 11,000 families living in barracks and other temporary quarters in Berlin in 1931, more than 43,000 families living in badly decayed pre-war buildings, and approximately 40,000 families living in unsuitable attics or basements.[6] The housing shortage remained one of the worst social problems. Despite a political atmosphere favorable to reform—at least at times during the twenties—the pioneering work of architects, planners and other reformers was denied fulfillment because of the disastrous fluctuations in the economy.

The lack of sufficient centralized control in carrying out the housing program and the resultant convulsions in housing production contributed to the unstable economic situation. Martin Wagner summed up these effects as follows: Government, which had to support unemployed building trades workers, suffered. Building materials producers, who had to take unpredictable risks in their pricing, suffered. Planners, architects and money managers, unable to make long-range plans, suffered. Bureaucrats, overrun by building corporations and architects during peak seasons, suffered. Housing placement bureaus and families with no dwelling of their own, suffered. But, perhaps above all, the level of rents suffered under these conditions. Had it been possible to keep the building industry regularly employed on a year-round basis, Wagner calculated, it would have been possible to reduce rents by fifteen percent.[7]

The public service building corporations continued their efforts to provide adequate housing for those least able to pay. But at the end of 1929 the administration of GEHAG complained that it was next to impossible to obtain first mortgages and that the high interest rates demanded by private lenders were resulting in a steady increase in rents.[8]

Another reason for the insufficiencies of the building program in Berlin was the highly complex bureaucratic system of the municipal administration, against which Wagner himself was powerless to act. The amount of red tape involved in obtaining a building permit was formidable. One anonymous critic claimed it cost an architect over 800 kilometers of travel to and from various offices in order to have one particular building permit finally approved. For even the smallest of projects these preliminaries involved some twenty-six different offices and could take from eight weeks to nine months to complete.[9]

It was a constant struggle for those organizations directly associated with the labor movement to continue to find the means to relieve the ever-present housing shortage. Once government support dwindled, the imbalance between rising rents and falling wages brought to an end any possibility of achieving the idealistic sociopolitical goals of the public benefit housing movement. Great efforts were made by these building organizations to offset the crippling effects of the worsening situation and to resist the tendency steadily to decrease the size of minimal dwelling units. During 1930 GEHAG was able to complete the construction of 3,046 units and to begin the construction of 1,812 more. For the year 1931 (the general financial crash hit Germany in July of 1931) these figures fell to 913 units completed and only 387 units begun. Construction ground to a halt.

From an architectural standpoint, as Ernst May observed, even competitions brought few surprises after 1928.[10] The essential principles had been developed, accepted and promulgated in the program of the *Reichsforschungsgesellschaft* competition for Haselhorst. Much attention was paid to reconsidering the floorplans of dwelling units, but this had relatively little impact on the basic arrangement of apartments. Similarly, the discussion of the supposed merits of high-rise housing also had little impact on workers' settlements around 1930. It seems that the enthusiasm for tall buildings in some circles had little to contribute to solving housing problems. Ernst May, for one, considered it merely a fad, calling it the "tall-building bacillus" which followed in the wake of the "skyscraper-office-building psychosis."[11]

Certainly the broad spectrum of statesmen, builders, planners, and architects who did the most to advance the cause of workers' housing—those who envisioned Berlin transformed into a new type of open, green metropolis—favored the concept of a wreath of low-density, low-rise settlements outside the older urbanized area. They would have preferred to see these consist primarily of single-family rowhouses.

The Greater Berlin Association for Small Housing *(Gross-Berliner Verein für Kleinwohnungswesen)* had been founded on the initiative of the Prussian government as early as 1912, with the explicit aim of creating a center to coordinate all efforts toward improving housing for lower income people.[12] Among the founders of this organization had been several great names: the planners Joseph Stübben and Theodor Goecke, as well as the representatives of two great industrial families in Berlin, Ernst von Borsig and Carl Friedrich von Siemens. The earliest efforts of this organization already had established the major directions pursued during the twenties. Following a period of intense activity after the war, which resulted in the establishment of the Housing Welfare Office *(Wohnungsfürsorgegesellschaft)* as its successor in 1919, the *Verein für Kleinwohnungswesen* had been inactive as a separate organization. The rapid collapse of the housing program in 1931, however, stimulated its revival in a last-stand effort to save the situation. This was impossible to do, yet the attempt served to document the concepts, the people and the organizations crucial to the program throughout the decade of the twenties.

In 1931 the board of directors of the Greater Berlin Association for Small Housing got together in an attempt to find financing to revivify housing construction. Included were representatives of the Ministry of Labor, the Welfare Ministry, the Prussian Parliament, the City of Berlin (including *Stadtbaurat* Wagner), the Housing Welfare Office (Jakob Schallenberger) GEHAG, and the *Deutsche Gartenstadtgesellschaft*. Representatives of credit institutions, the Association of Socialized Building Trades, and other organizations also contributed. Architects on the board included Bruno Ahrends, who had helped design the *Gross-Siedlung Reinickendorf;* Friedrich Paulsen, editor of *Die Bauwelt;* and Bruno Taut. Their most important goal, they said, was to promote low-rise settlements at the urban periphery, and these were to consist primarily of single-family rowhouses. They hoped to reverse the current trends toward minimal dwellings in four or five-story walk-ups, which by 1930 had become the norm because of extremely tight money. Unfortunately, their attempt could not succeed.

The reader may recall that one of the most significant early steps in transforming housing had been radical revision of the building code. The pattern of growth during the twenties indicated that Berlin would increase in population from four million to some ten million during the next sixty years. Based on the revised building code, Martin Wagner predicted that this increase would be housed as follows: forty percent in five-story walk-ups, seventeen percent in four-story buildings, sixteen percent in three-story, and twenty-seven percent in two-story houses.[13] Such development offered the prospect of an open, low-density city requiring planning on a scale untried up to that time. In 1931 it was regretted in the *Verein für Kleinwohnungswesen* that the percentage of dwellings built as two-story houses in Berlin had reached twenty-seven percent only in 1925 and had dropped steadily thereafter to a low of five percent in 1930.[14] Thus economics had denied realization of the goals envisioned by the building code, even though the modern *Gross-Siedlungen* here presented did keep density within limits. No high-rise housing at all was built in Berlin during the twenties, nor, indeed, until after 1950. Some people now are convinced that tall buldings have proven unsuitable as housing and that the arguments of planners in the twenties on this point were correct after all.

A characteristic shift in the reformers' concepts of realizable workers' housing during the twenties can be seen by comparing Mebes & Emmerich's *Siedlung Heidehof* of 1923–24 with their *Friedrich Ebert Siedlung* of 1929–30. Heidenhof, simple in form, yet so quaintly romantic in conception, had been designed in a red brick vernacular style as a miniature agricultural village clustered about a square and radiating individual gardens of the "villagers." Everything was intimate in scale, and the fundamental intention was to solve the housing problems of urban workers by getting them away from those problems. The back-to-the-land movement had had distinctly anti-urban tendencies, which precluded its providing the ultimate answer to the housing problems of large cities. A settlement such as *Heidehof* could only be an interesting form of suburban housing, just one part of a many-facetted solution.

The *Gross-Siedlungen,* such as Mebes & Emmerich's *Friedrich Ebert Stadt,* represented a frontal attack on the problems of workers' housing in cities. This meant, first of all, efficient organization and large-scale planning and research at all levels of the design process. For economy's sake it meant a stripping down to essentials and a clear recognition of the fundamental nature of the problems. It also often meant that rationalized forms and methods had to be developed which might conflict with the traditional living patterns of the working class. In short, the *Gross-Siedlungen* were the modern architects' expression of New Objectivity or *Neue Sachlichkeit* in housing.

The stripping down characteristic of *Neue Sachlichkeit* became synonymous with *Neues Bauen.* It was most apparent in the outward appearance of the buildings. Architectonic forms came to be treated as elemental statements of basic functions: the house as a container, the roof as a lid, walls as envelopes to keep out the elements. While this process of reduction was strongly influenced by formalistic considerations almost inevitably resulting in the selection of simple, geometric shapes, there was a genuine spirit of searching to find paradigmatic solutions to clearly stated problems. A great amount of thought went into the planning of these settlements down to the last detail. Behind the sometimes seemingly stark forms lay a sensitivity to human values coupled with an impatience to forge ahead in organizing a new way of living.

Of course, there were also less than favorable reactions to this new type of dwelling and the visions for a new life. New Objectivity occasionally was greeted as "New and Idiotic Objectivity," as in a piece by Werner Hegemann. There he touched upon the hurdles architects faced when they tried to restructure society through architecture, to prepare people for a new life they perhaps were not ready for.[15] He wrote that the romantic dreams of the builders of modernist housing almost always collapsed afterwards, because, although frantic, homeless people did move into these futuristic new buildings, it was almost always *only* such people who did... in his view. People whose furniture, pictures, lifestyle, and ideals were resolutely rooted in well established habits of yesterday were not ready to be convinced by reason, and certainly not by a "romanticism of engineering." Such, too, were among the problems of the new architecture.

On that note we may terminate this recounting of the part of the German revolution in workers' housing that took place in Berlin during the 1920s. One primary conclusion stands out: the new architecture was in its essence not a matter of esthetics but of social politics. The politics of inspired but pragmatic socialism played the most important role of all. Of course, the politics of action and the politics of administration were engaged in by people who belonged to a variety of political parties. Clearly the liberal social policies and attitudes of the Social Democratic Party during the Weimar Republic were crucial, but during this period of privation and revolution in housing, political conservatives were also often social liberals when it came to this fundamental need of society.

Architecture was used as a dynamic force to improve the quality of life for a broad segment of the populace. Never before had idealistic social attitudes so profoundly transformed housing in so brief a time for so many. Although time and money were too short to realize all that had been envisioned, the transformation was nonetheless drastic, a revolution in housing for the working class in a major metropolis.

## Epilogue

In view of the enormous changes—social, political, and physical—that have taken place in Berlin since the early thirties, one would certainly be curious about what happened to these housing projects durng the intervening decades. Were they changed under Hitler's rule? Were they destroyed during the Second World War? What has happened to them since the war?

The advent of the National Socialist regime in 1933 meant a radical shift away from the policies of the Social Democrats. In the field of housing the new policies meant de-emphasizing the construction of modern housing developments in major cities in favor of emphasizing "inner colonization," i.e., settling the underdeveloped rural areas of Germany. The concept of back-to-the-land was revived, especially for the chronically unemployed, and countless settlements of rudimentary small houses—with their characteristic steeply pitched roofs and pieces of land to till—sprang up, adding a *Siedler Strasse,* it seemed, to every town and village across Germany. For Berlin and other large cities, the Nazi era often meant looking to an old answer for the housing shortage.

Existing living space in large homes and pre-1914 apartment buildings was redistributed by dividing it into multiple small dwelling units. The public benefit building corporations were taken over by Hitler's *Arbeiter-Front* and were required to devote their energies to new building in areas generally away from the major urban centers. When it came to housing, the Nazis apparently had a distinctly anti-urban attitude. Yet, although many of the most advanced housing projects of the twenties were criticized for their "un-German" or "Bolshevist" appearance, the fact remained that these *Siedlungen* were assets to Berlin, no matter who was in power. Thus, as physical entities the settlements remained as they had been built. Apparently there were no attempts to any significance to make changes in the physical character or appearance of the *Siedlungen,* although the social spirit and interaction intended were effectively hindered under the new management.

The Second World War had a catastrophic impact on Berlin. Aerial bombing attacks began in the spring of 1943 and did not end until April of 1945, when the Russians began to encircle and attack the city by land. Since Hitler had ordered an all-out, last-ditch defense, much of what had not been hit in the bombing was destroyed by artillery and fire in the assault that culminated in the surrender of the city on May 2, 1945. In the resulting vast wasteland of rubble, thirty-five percent of all housing had been totally destroyed and at least another thirty-five percent damaged to a serious extent.

The first task after the war was to clear the rubble and to take provisional measures to house the homeless and the steady stream of refugees. But Berlin's second great housing crisis of the twentieth century is a different story. Suffice it to say that it was not possible to begin a new housing program until after the allied airlift of 1948–49 had succeeded in breaking the eleven-month Soviet blockade of the city. During the interim, while many areas were simply bulldozed to await later development, most of the *Siedlungen* of the twenties could be saved. Since they were located at some distance from the center of the city, the projects presented here were away from the zone of heaviest damage. All of them have been rebuilt.

The *Siedlung Lindenhof* was among the hardest hit during the war and, among the projects discussed in this study, is the one which has experienced the most significant changes in the course of rebuilding. As mentioned in the discussion of Lindenhof, Bruno Taut's bachelors' billet was not rebuilt, and new housing was added, raising the site density. Taut's *Siedlung Schillerpark* also had new housing added in the 1950s. Otherwise, the workers' housing projects of the twenties today present very much the impression their designers originally intended. Generally restored in their physical fabric during the 1950s, almost all of them have enjoyed further renovation since the 1970s. Following a period of a lack of understanding for the esthetic intentions of the designers and a period of self-expression among the residents (e.g., rather individualistic treatments of the entrances of the rowhouses at Onkel Toms Hütte), these developments—in West Berlin, at least—are now protected by historic preservation regulations and are being restored to their original colors in keeping with careful research. Lavish vegetation is the primary change from these projects' appearance when they were new, but that is one change, we can be sure, which is entirely in keeping with the architects' original intentions.

Workers' housing from the 1920s continues to fare well in Berlin more than half a century after it was built. When compared with the record of some

# Notes

**Key to Abbreviations:**

BG       *Die Baugilde* (Berlin)

BW      *Die Bauwelt* (Berlin)

Form    *Die Form* (Berlin)

NB       *Der Neubau* (Berlin)

StB      *Der Städtebau* (Berlin)

StBK    *Stadtbaukunst alter und neuer Zeit* (Berlin)

StBV    *Städtebauliche Vorträge* (Berlin)

VW      *Die Volkswohnung* (Berlin)

WLB    *Wasmuths Lexikon der Baukunst* (Berlin)

WMB    *Wasmuths Monatshefte für Baukunst* (Berlin)

## Chapter 1

1. Werner Hegemann, "Bücherschau," *Stadtbaukunst,* 21(1926), pp. 15–16.
2. Catherine Bauer, *Modern Housing* (Boston and New York: Houghton Mifflin, 1934), 16.
3. Hugo Schulze and Alfred Dallmann, *50 Jahre Kampf gegen die Mietskaserne* (Berlin: Baugenossenschaft Freie Scholle, 1947), p. 3.
4. Paul von Breitenbach, "Runderlass betreffend Förderung von Kleinhaussiedlungen und Kleinhausbauten...." *Centralblatt der Bauverwaltung,* 37(1917), pp. 201–4.
5. Martin Wagner, "Offener Brief an Herrn Kommerzienrat Haberland," *Die Volkswohnung,* 1(1919), pp. 285–86; and Georg Haberland, "Offener Brief an Herrn Dr. Ing. Martin Wagner," ibid., pp. 312–13, which is followed by Wagner's counterreply.
6. The first definitive translation of Sitte's book into English was prepared by George R. Collins and Christiane C. Collins, who also wrote a thorough analysis of Sitte's work and its influences, entitled *Camillo Sitte and the Birth of Modern City Planning* (New York: Random House, 1965).
7. For information on the history of housing reform see Bruno Schwan, "Wohnungsreform," in Albrecht, *Handwörterbuch,* pp. 836–38, and Rose von Mangoldt, "Wohnungsreform," *WLB,* 5, pp. 618–20.

8. See "Bodenreform," *Meyers Lexikon,* pp. 571–73.
9. Adolf Damaschke, *Die Bodenreform: Grundsätzliches und Geschichtliches zur Erkenntnis und Überwindung der sozialen Not* (seventh edition, Jena: Gustav Fischer, 1912).
10. Leberecht Migge, "Neues Gartenbauen," in Erwin Gutkind et al., *Neues Bauen: Grundlagen zur praktischen Siedlungstätigkeit* (Berlin: Bauwelt, 1919), p. 104.
11. See Gerhard Albrecht, "Gartenstadtbewegung," in Albrecht, *Handwörterbuch,* pp. 262–66; Hans Kampffmeyer, *"Die Gartenstadtbewegung* (second edition, Leipzig: Teubner, 1913); and Hermann Salomon, "Gartenstädte," *StBV,* 6(1913).
12. Albert Gut, "Das Wohnungswesen in Deutschland seit dem Weltkriege," in Stübben, *Hundert Jahre Architekten-Verein zu Berlin, 1824–1924,* pp. 63–77. Relative legislation is also discussed by Rolf Spörhase, "Wohnungsunternehmen im Rahmen staatlicher Wohnungspolitik," in his *Wohnungsunternehmen im Wandel der Zeit* (Hamburg: Sachse, 1947), pp. 88–90; and by Otto Wolz, "Parlament und Wohnungsfrage," in Albrecht, *Handwörterbuch,* pp. 583–88.

**Chapter 2**

1. Bruno Taut, *Die Auflösung der Städte* (Hagen: Volkwang, 1920).
2. Werner Hegemann, *Das steinerne Berlin: Geschichte der grössten Mietskasernenstadt der Welt* (Berlin: Kiepenheuer, 1930; reprinted Berlin: Ullstein, 1963).
3. Hans Luckhardt, circular letter of March 30, 1920, from the "Utopian Correspondence" of the Glass Chain group around Bruno Taut. Reprinted in English in the translation by Christiane C. Collins and George R. Collins of Ulrich Conrads and Hans G. Sperlich, *The Architecture of Fantasy* (New York: Praeger, 1962), p. 144.
4. Bruno Taut, *Auflösung,* plate 12.
5. Ibid., text, p. 1.
6. Ibid., plate 4.
7. Bruno Taut, "Die Erde eine gute Wohnung," *VW,* 1(1919), pp. 45–48.
8. My colleague from Columbia University, Rosemarie Bletter, is preparing a book on Taut. See also the bibliography, especially Iain Boyd Whyte, *Bruno Taut and the Architecture of Activism* (Cambridge: Cambridge University, 1982).
9. Bruno Taut, "Alte Bauweisen in neuzeitlicher Form," *VW,* 1(1919), pp. 69–70.
10. Heinz Johannes, *Neues Bauen in Berlin* (Berlin: Deutscher Kunstverlag, 1931).
11. Adolf Scheidt, in Erwin Gutkind et al., *Neues Bauen: Grundlagen zur praktischen Siedlungstätigkeit* (Berlin: Bauwelt, 1919), 7.

**Chapter 3**

1. For commentary see Schallenberger and Kraffert, *Berliner Wohnungsbauten,* p. 5.
2. A competition to design a regional plan was opened in December 1908, closed in December 1909, and judged in March 1910. Hermann Jansen won first place, and the principal runners-up were the team of Joseph Brix and Felix Genzmer (leaders of the *Städtebauliche Vorträge* at the *Technische Hochschule* in Charlottenburg) and the team of Rudolf Eberstadt, Bruno Möhring, and Richard Petersen. These designs had great impact in the development of city planning for Berlin and should be the subject of further study. Representative illustrations are in Gustav Adolf Platz, *Die Baukunst der neuesten Zeit* (Berlin: Propyläen, 1927), pp. 483, 492 and 500.
3. For a history of the Berlin building codes see Heinz Ehrlich, *Die Berliner Bauordnungen: ihre wichtigsten Bauvorschriften und deren Einfluss auf den Wohnungsbau der Stadt Berlin* (Dissertation, Berlin, Jena: Neuenhan, 1933).

4. Wagner's dissertation was published as *Städtische Freiflächenpolitik* (Berlin: Heymann, 1915).

5. See Gustav Böss, "Die Verwaltungsgemeinde Berlin und ihre Aufgaben," in Fritz Elsas et al., *Die Deutschen Städte, ihre Arbeit von 1918 bis 1928* (Berlin: Deutscher Kommunal Verlag, 1928), pp. 6–8.

6. Jakob Schallenberger was the principal figure guiding the administration of the *Wohnungsfürsorgegesellschaft*. For a report on housing built in Berlin up to 1926 with the support of public funds see Jakob Schallenberger and Hans Kraffert, *Berliner Wohnungsbauten aus öffentlichen Mitteln* (Berlin: Bauwelt, 1926).

7. Rudolf Eberstadt in his *Handbuch des Wohnungswesens und der Wohnungsfrage* (fourth edition, Jena: Gustav Fischer, 1920) was a pioneer in demonstrating the evils of the older tenements. For plans and examples see his book as well as Adolf Behne, *Neues Wohnen, neues Bauen* (Leipzig: Hesse & Becker, 1927). An excellent summary, with illustrations from both of the above, is to be found in Friedrich Schmidt, "Geschichte der Wohnung," in Albrecht, *Handwörterbuch*, pp. 274–88.

8. Catherine Bauer, *Modern Housing*, p. 188.

9. Bruno Taut, *Die Stadtkrone* (Jena: Eugen Diederichs, 1919), pp. 63–64.

10. The historical background is discussed in Bauer, *Modern Housing*, p. 79; Willi Baumgarten, "Baugenossenschaften," in Albrecht, *Handwörterbuch*, pp. 49–56; Hugo Schulze and Adolf Dallman, "Die Gründung der Baugenossenschaften," in *50 Jahre Kampf gegen die Mietskaserne*, p. 4; and Verband Berliner Wohnungsbaugenossenschaften und -gesellschaften e.V., *Geschichte der gemeinnützigen Wohnungswirtschaft in Berlin* (Berlin: privately printed, 1947). See also Hegemann, *Der Städtebau*, pp. 10ff; Hegemann, *Das steinerne Berlin*, pp. 200–06; and "Baugenossenschaften" in *WLB*, 5, pp. 67–69.

11. There are two books documenting GAGFAH: Hans Bechly et al., *16,000 Wohnungen für Angestellte* (Berlin: Wasmuth, 1928); and Hermann Wandersleb et al., *GAGFAH 1918–1968* (Hamburg: Hammonia, 1968), which includes a facsimile of Bechly's *Die Heimstätte des Angestellten*.

12. See *Geschichte der gemeinnützigen Wohnungswirtschaft in Berlin* (Berlin: Verband Berliner Wohungsbaugenossenschaften und -gesellschaften e.V., 1957) and "Gewerkschaften und Wohnungsbau," in Hermann Wandersleb et al., *Handwörterbuch des Städtebaues, Wohnungs- und Siedlungswesens* (three volumes, Stuttgart: Kohlhammer, 1959).

13. For a summary of the work of GEHAG see its *Festschrift*, Gemeinnützige Heimstätten Aktiengesellschaft, *GEHAG, 1924–1957: Entstehung eines gewerkschaftlichen Wohnungsunternehmens* (Berlin: GEHAG, 1957).

14. See *GEHAG, 1924–1957*, pp. 11ff.

15. See Martin Wagner, "Regie," *BW*, 21(1930), pp. 801–2. In 1985 for the one hundredth anniversary of Wagner's birth, Achim Wendschuh and Lodovica Scarpa are planning a Wagner exhibition at the *Akademie der Künste* in Berlin.

16. Max Jahn, "Architektur und Sozialismus," *BG*, 8(1926), pp. 809–10.

**Chapter 4**

1. In addition to various articles in *BG, BW, StB* and *WMB*, Klein published his system as "Beiträge zur Wohnungsfrage," in Block, *Probleme des Bauens*, pp. 116–45. It is from the latter that the presentation here has been abstracted.

2. Werner Hegemann, "Schmitthenner, Bruno Taut, usw.: Sklaven eines falsch verstandenen Klassizismus?" *WMB*, 12(1928), pp. 345–48.

## Chapter 5

1. Internationale Kongresse für neues Bauen und Städtisches Hochbauamt in Frankfurt am Main, *Die Wohnung für das Existenzminimum* (Frankfurt: Englert & Schlosser, 1930).
2. See "Reichs-Forschungs-Gesellschaft für Bau und Wohnung," [*sic*] *BW*, 18(1927), p. 685.
3. Ernst May, "Die Wohnung für das Existenzminimum," Internationale Kongresse, *Die Wohnung für das Existenzminimum*, pp. 10–16.
4. Walter Gropius, "Die soziologischen Grundlagen der Minimalwohnung für die städtische Bevölkerung," Internationale Kongresse, *Die Wohnung für das Existenzminimum*, pp. 17–19.
5. Taut, *Bauen: der neue Wohnbau* (Leipzig, Berlin: Klinkhardt & Biermann, 1927), p. 46.
6. Martin Wagner, "Aufgaben im Berliner Wohnungsbau," *BW*, 19(1928), pp. 1129–31.
7. Taut, *Bauen: der neue Wohnbau*, p. 46.
8. Fritz Beuster, Erich Leyser and Jakob Schallenberger, *Wohnungspolitik von Gestern und Morgen* (Berlin: Gross-Berliner Verein für Kleinwohnungswesen, 1931), p. 17.
9. Internationaler Verband für Wohnungswesen, *Die sozialpolitische Bedeutung der Wohnungswirtschaft in Gegenwart und Zukunft* (Frankfurt: Internationaler Verband für Wohnungswesen, 1931).
10. Ibid., p. 159.
11. Ibid., pp. 118–22.
12. Ibid., p. 127.
13. Ibid., p. 160.
14. Ludwig Hilberseimer, "Die Wohnung unserer Zeit," *Form*, 6(1931), p. 250.

## Chapter 6

1. For a discussion of this settlement in the contemporary literature see Fritz Stahl, "Die Gartenstadt Staaken," *WMB*, 3(1918/19), pp. 137–98.
2. For a discussion of the *Siedlung an der Lentze Allee* in the contemporary literature see Walter Lehwess, "Kleinhassiedlung in Berlin Dahlem," *StBK*, 2(1921), pp. 213–20.
3. For a discussion of the *Siedlung Lindenhof* in the contemporary literature see Paul Wolf, *Wohnung und Siedlung* (Berlin: Wasmuth, n.d. [ca. 1920]), pp. 211–13.
4. These principles were drawn together in Raymond Unwin's book *Town Planning in Practice*, which had been translated into German by 1910 as *Grundlagen des Städtebaues* (Berlin: Baumgärtel, 1910). A second, enlarged and revised edition appeared in 1922 and a thin volume of additions—which included Unwin's lecture on "Nothing Gained by Overcrowding"—was published in 1930.
5. For Taut's own discussion of this building see Bruno Taut, "Ein Ledigenheim in Schöneberg," *StBK*, 1(1920), pp. 136–38. Destroyed in the Second World War, Taut's building was not rebuilt.
6. For a contemporary discussion of the developments that had preceded the building of the *Siedlung Tempelhofer Feld* see "Das Tempelhofer Feld," *VW*, 2(1920), pp. 202–03.
7. Taut, *Bauen: der neue Wohnbau*, p. 4.
8. For the results of the competition held for the design of these buildings see Werner Hegemann, "Randbebauung des Tempelhofer Feldes," *WMB*, 9(1925), pp. 205–8.
9. For the architect's own presentation of these concepts see Eduard Jobst Siedler, "Heimstättengärten in der Gross-Stadt," in Fritz Block et al., *Probleme des Bauens: der Wohnbau* (Potsdam: Müller & Kiepenhauer, 1928), pp. 47–54.
10. This settlement should not be confused with the later and more famous *Gross-Siedlung Siemensstadt*. For a discussion of Hertlein's project in the contemporary literature see

"Neue Bauten der Siedlung Siemensstadt," *WMB*, 14(1930), pp. 186–88, which includes the original portion as well as the later expansion.

11. For a discussion of the *Siedlung Heidehof* in the contemporary literature see Jakob Schallenberger and Hans Kraffert, *Berliner Wohnungsbauten aus öffentlichen Mitteln* (Berlin: Bauwelt, 1926), pp. 48–52. A contemporary color rendering appears in Albert Gut and others, *Der Wohnungsneubau in Deutschland nach dem Weltkriege* (Munich: Bruckmann, 1928), plate X.

12. For a discussion of *Siedlung Schillerpark* in the contemporary literature see Jakob Schallenberger, *Der Wohnungsneubau in Berlin* (Berlin: Berliner Wohnungsfürsorgegesellschaft, n.d.), pp. 5–6.

13. For a discussion of the *Siedlung Ceciliengärten* in the planner's own book see Paul Wolf, *Wohnung und Siedlung*, pp. 191–205.

14. Paul Wolf, *Städtebau: das Formproblem der Stadt in Vergangenheit und Zukunft* (Leipzig: Klinkhardt & Biermann, 1919).

15. For a discussion of the *Hufeisen Siedlung* in the contemporary literature see Leo Adler, "Siedlungen in Britz," *WMB*, 11(1927), pp. 35–90.

16. For contemporary comments on disadvantages resulting from Taut's form above practicality see Adler, "Siedlungen in Britz," pp. 386–89, and Werner Hegemann, "Dachüberstand, Frostschäden und Kritik der 'rationalen Vernunft' Bruno Tauts," *WMB*, 11(1927), p. 463.

17. Taut, *Bauen: der neue Wohnbau*, p. 47. It is fortunate that a published colored rendering preserves the original impression of the streets of row houses at Britz as Taut envisioned them. See Gut, *Wohnungsneubauten in Deutschland nach dem Weltkriege*, plate XI. It is also fortunate that Taut's projects are undergoing a second wave of preservation since the Second World War, in which an attempt is being made to restore the original colors.

18. For a discussion of the DEGEWO *Siedlung* in Britz in the contemporary literature, see Adler, "Siedlungen in Britz," pp. 385–89, and "1000 Wohnungen: Siedlung in Britz," *BW*, 18(1927), Heft 9. For a contemporary color rendering of the *Siedlung* see Gut, *Wohnungsneubauten in Deutschland*, plate XII.

19. For a discussion of this residential complex in the contemporary literature see Walter Curt Behrendt, "Neue Wohngruppe der Architekten Paul Mebes und Paul Emmerich, Berlin," *NB*, 9(1927), pp. 3–12.

20. For a monograph on the housing of Paul Mebes see Edina Meyer, *Paul Mebes: Miethausbau in Berlin, 1906–38* (Berlin: Richard Seitz, 1972).

21. It is worth noting that it had been W.C. Behrendt who published a book on unified facades: W.C. Behrendt, *Die einheitliche Blockfront als Raumelement im Stadtbau* (Berlin: Ernst Cassirer, 1911).

22. For a presentation of this *Siedlung* in the contemporary literature see Georg Stein, "Neue Strassenbahnsiedlung mit Betriebsbahnhof in der Müllerstrasse,, Berlin N.," *NB*, 9(1927), pp. 261–64.

23. For a discussion of this *Siedlung* in the contemporary literature see Werner Hegemann, "Wohnhausgruppe der GAGFAH . . . in Lichterfelde," *WMB*, 11(1927), pp. 425–29.

24. For an illustration of the Möhring, Eberstadt and Petersen design see Gustav Adolf Platz, *Baukunst der neuesten Zeit* (Berlin: Propyläen, 1927), p. 500.

25. For a discussion of this *Siedlung*, also known as *Siedlung Onkel Toms Hütte, GEHAG-Siedlung Zehlendorf*, or *Waldsiedlung Zehlendorf*, in the contemporary literature, see Adolf Behne, "Die Zehlendorfer Siedlung der GEHAG," *Form*, 4(1929), pp. 4–8; and Alexander Schwab, "Zur GEHAG-Siedlung Zehlendorf: Grundsätzliches und Wirtschaftliches," ibid., pp. 8–14.

26.  For insight into this process and reaction to it see Eduard Jobst Siedler, "Ein Gross-Siedlungs-Vorhaben in Zehlendorf," *BG,* 8(1926), pp. 956ff, and Bruno Taut, Jakob Schallenberger, and Hans Kraffert, "Erklärung zur Siedlung der GEHAG in Zehlendorf," ibid., pp. 1017–18.

27.  See Leberecht Migge, *Die Gartenkultur des 20. Jahrhunderts* (Jena: Eugen Diederichs, 1913), reprinted ca. 1980.

28.  Behne, *Form,* 4(1929), pp. 5–6.

## Chapter 7

1.  Martin Wagner, "Aufgaben im Berliner Wohnungsbau," *BW,* 19(1928), pp. 1129–31; and Walter Gropius, "Der Berliner Wohnungsbau," ibid., pp. 1149–51.

2.  Reichsforschungsgesellschaft für Wirtschaftlichkeit im Bau- und Wohnungswesen e.V., *Reichswettbewerb zur Erlangung von Vorentwürfen für die Aufteilung und Bebauung des Geländes der Forschungssiedlung in Spandau-Haselhorst* (Berlin: Reichsforschungsgesell-schaft, 1929), p. 20.

3.  For a discussion of prizewinning designs other than the Gropius-Fischer proposals see Friedrich Paulsen, "Der Wettbewerb der Reichsforschung," *BW,* 20(1929), pp. 137–42.

4.  For the best contemporary discussion of this *Siedlung* see "Gross-Siedlung Siemensstadt," *BW,* 21(1930), Heft 46, and "Gross-Siedlung Siemensstadt, Bebauung am Göbelplatz und am Geislerpfad, 1930–31," *BW,* 22(1931), Heft 47.

5.  Werner Hegemann, "Martin Wagner gewinnt Scharoun," *WMB,* 13(1929), p. 84.

6.  "Architektenvereinigung 'Der Ring'," *Form,* 1(1926), p. 225.

7.  When I asked Professor Scharoun in the summer of 1965 about the possible influence of mechanistic oceanliner forms on his architecture, he goodnaturedly replied, "Well, I *did* grow up in Bremen, after all."

8.  For a discussion of this settlement in the contemporary literature see "GEHAG Gross-Siedlung Carl Legien Stadt an der Carmen Sylva Strasse," *BW,* 22(1931), Heft 19.

9.  For a thorough presentation and discussion of this settlement in the contemporary literature see "Gross-Siedlung Berlin Reinickendorf, Schiller-Promenade," *BW,* 21(1930), Heft 48.

10.  Adolf Behne, *Neues Wohnen, Neues Bauen* (Leipzig: Hesse & Becker, 1927).

11.  For a discussion of these buildings, see Johannes, *Neues Bauen in Berlin,* pp. 89d, e, and g.

12.  For a discussion of this settlement in the contemporary literature see Paul Mebes, "Die Friedrich Ebert Siedlung in Berlin," *WMB,* 16(1932), pp. 429–35. It was commissioned by the *Eintracht Gemeinnützige Wohnungsbau A.G.*

13.  For a discussion of this *Siedlung* in the contemporary literature see Paul Mebes, "Die Feuer- und Rauchlose Siedlung in Berlin-Steglitz," *WMB,* 16(1932), pp. 115–22.

14.  For a discussion of this settlement in the contemporary literature see Werner Hegemann, "Siedlung Heimat in Berlin-Siemensstadt," *WMB,* 14(1930), pp. 537–41.

15.  Ibid., p. 537.

16.  For a discussion of this *Siedlung* in the contemporary literature see Ulf Dietrich, "Neuer Betriebsbahnhof und Wohnbauten der Berliner Strassenbahn," *WMB,* 14(1930), pp. 577–82.

17.  The Britz project, designed and built in the early thirties, was presented in *WMB,* 16(1932), pp. 73–77, but will not be discussed here.

18.  Walter Gropius, *Scope of Total Architecture* (New York: Harper, 1955).

19.  It is interesting that Gropius made a serious attempt at conditioning professional opinion in favor of his competition design in the previously cited article of ostensibly general, theoretical interest, entitled "Der Berliner Wohnungsbau," published just one month prior to the judging of the RFG competition. After the judging Gropius published his competition

designs in *Bauwelt*. See Walter Gropius, "Das Ergebnis des Reichsforschungs-Wettbewerbes," *BW,* 20(1929), pp. 158–62.

20. The same photos of Muche's drawing and Breuer's model are illustrated in Herbert Bayer, Walter Gropius and Ise Gropius, *Bauhaus: 1919–1928* (Boston: Branford, 1952), p. 76, and Württembergischer Kunstverein, *50 Jahre Bauhaus* (Stuttgart: Württembergischer Kunstverein, 1968), p. 83.
21. Marcel Breuer, "Beiträge zur Frage des Hochhauses," *Form,* 5(1930), pp. 113–17.
22. Ludwig Hilberseimer, "Die Wohnung unserer Zeit," *Form,* 6(1931), pp. 249–70.

## Chapter 8

1. Beuster, *Wohnungspolitik,* p. 23.
2. For a contemporary comment on the conditions see Alexander Schwab, "Zur GEHAG-Siedlung Zehlendorf," *Form,* 4(1929), pp. 8–14.
3. For a summary of the financial aspects of the public housing program see Bauer, *Modern Housing,* pp. 270–81, and Otto Lehmann, "Hauszinssteuerhypothek," in Albrecht, *Handwörterbuch,* pp. 347–53.
4. Beuster, Leyser and Schallenberger, *Wohnungspolitik,* p. 19.
5. Wagner, "Aufgaben im Berliner Wohnungsbau," p. 1131.
6. Beuster, Leyser and Schallenberger, *Wohnungspolitik,* p. 23.
7. Wagner, "Aufgaben im Berliner Wohnungsbau," p. 1131.
8. See *GEHAG, 1924–1957,* p. 17.
9. Among the most interesting discussions of over-administration are Martin Wagner, "Aufgaben im Berliner Wohnungsbau," p. 1131; "Die schleppende Genehmigung von Bauentwürfen," *BW* (1929), pp. 452ff; and E. Runge, "Die Erschwerung der Siedlungstätigkeit," ibid., pp. 533–35.
10. Ernst May, "Städtebauliche Fortschritte," Frankfurter Zeitung, Feb. 2, 1929, pp. 1–2.
11. Ernst May and Walter Gropius, "Flachbau-Hochbau," *Form,* 4(1929), p. 672.
12. A summary of the work of this organization is in Beuster, Leyser and Schallenberger, *Wohnungspolitik,* pp. 2–8.
13. Wagner, "Aufgaben im Berliner Wohnungsbau," p. 1129.
14. Beuster et al., *Wohnungspolitik,* p. 19.
15. Werner Hegemann, "'Neue' und 'idiotische' 'Sachlichkeit'," *WMB,* 12(1928), p. 374.

# Selected Bibliography

## Abbreviations

BAW     *Berliner Architekturwelt* (Berlin)
BG      *Die Baugilde* (Berlin)
BM     *Der Baumeister* (Berlin)
BW     *Bauwelt* (Berlin)
CBB    *Centralblatt der Bauverwaltung* (Berlin)
DB     *Deutsche Bauzeitung* (Berlin)
Form   *Die Form* (Berlin)
JRIBA  *Journal of the Royal Institute of British Architects* (London)
MB     *Moderne Bauformen* (Stuttgart)
NB     *Der Neubau* (Berlin)
StB    *Der Städtebau* (Berlin)
StBK   *Stadtbaukunst Alter und Neuer Zeit* (Berlin)
StBV   *Städtebauliche Vorträge* (Berlin)
VW     *Die Volkswohnung* (Berlin)
WLB   *Wasmuths Lexikon der Baukunst* (Berlin)
WMB  *Wasmuths Monatshefte für Baukunst* (Berlin)
ZfB    *Zeitschrift für Bauwesen* (Berlin)

## General Information

Akademie der Künste. *Arbeitsrat für Kunst 1918–1921* (exhibition catalog). Berlin: Akademie der Künste, 1980.

Akademie der Künste. *Bauen in Berlin 1900–1964* (exhibition catalog). Berlin Akademie der Künste, 1964.

Akademie für Raumforschung und Landesplanung. *Handwörterbuch der Raumforschung und Raumordnung.* Hannover: Jänicke, 1966.

"Architektenvereinigung 'Der Ring'." *Form*, I (1926), 225.

Aronovici, Carol, ed. *America Can't Have Housing.* New York: The Museum of Modern Art, 1934.

Asmus, Gesine, et al. *Hinterhof, Keller und Mansarde: Einblicke in Berliner Wohnungselend 1901–1920.* Reinbeck bei Hamburg: Rowohlt, 1982.

Banham, Reyner. *Theory and Design of the First Machine Age.* New York: Frederick A. Praeger, 1960.

"Baugenossenschaften." *WLB*, V.

Baumgarten, Willi. "Baugenossenschaften." Albrecht, *Handwörterbuch,* 49–56.

Bayer, Herbert, Walter Gropius and Ise Gropius. *Bauhaus 1919–1928.* Boston: Charles R. Branford, 1952.

Behne, Adolf. *Der Moderne Zweckbau.* Berlin: Drei Masken Verlag, 1925. Reprint: Berlin, Frankfurt, Vienna: 1964.

Behne, Adolf. *Ruf zum Bauen.* Berlin: Wasmuth, 1920.

Benton, Tim, et al. *Design 1920s.* Milton Keynes: Open University Press, 1975.

Bentom, Tim. *The New Objectivity.* Milton Keynes: Open University Press, 1975.

Bletter, Rosemarie Haag. "Expressionism and the New Objectivity." *Art Journal,* vol. 43, no. 2 (Summer 1983), 108–20.

Brennert, Hans, and Erwin Stein, eds. *Probleme der neuen Stadt Berlin: Darstellungen der Zukunftsaufgaben einer Viermillionenstadt.* Berlin-Friedenau: Deutscher Kommunal-Verlag, 1926.

Collins, Christiane C. "Concerned Planning and Design: the Urban Experiment of Germany in the 1920s," in Frank D. Hirschbach et al, *Germany in the Twenties,* 30–47.

Conrads, Ulrich. *Programs and Manifestoes on 20th Century Architecture.* Cambridge: The MIT Press, 1970.

Conrads, Ulrich, and Hans G. Sperlich. *The Architecture of Fantasy.* Translated, edited, and expanded by Christiane C. Collins and George R. Collins, New York: Frederick A. Praeger, 1962.

Elsässer, Martin, et al. *Handbuch moderner Architektur, eine Kunstgeschichte der Architektur unsere Zeit.* Berlin: Safari, 1957.

Elsas, Fritz, et al. *Die deutschen städte, ihre arbeit von 1918 bis 1928.* Berlin: Deutscher Kommunal-Verlag, 1928.

de Fries, Heinrich. *Junge Baukunst in Deutschland.* Berlin: Stollberg, 1926.

Gay, Peter. *Weimar Culture: the Outsider as Insider.* New York: Harper & Row, 1968.

Gropius, Walter. *Scope of Total Architecture.* New York: Harper, 1955.

Gutkind, Erwin, et al. *Neues Bauen: Grundlagen zur praktischen Siedlungstätigkeit.* Berlin: Bauwelt, 1919.

Hajos, E.M., and Lepold Zahn. *Berliner Architektur der Nachkriegszeit.* Berlin: Albertus, 1928.

Halperin, S. William. *Germany Tried Democracy.* New York: W.W. Norton, 1965.

Hegemann, Werner. " 'Neue' und 'Idiotische' 'Sachlichkeit': Opernumbau und Wohnungsnot." *WMB,* XII (1928), 374.

Hegemann, Werner. *Reihenhaus-Fassaden: Geschäfts- und Wohnhäuser aus alter und neuer Zeit.* Berlin: Wasmuth, 1929.

Hennig-Schefold, Monica, and Inge Schaefer. *Frühe Moderne in Berlin.* Winterthur: Werk, 1967.

Hilberseimer, Ludwig. *Berliner Architektur der 20er Jahre.* Mainz and Berlin: Florian Kupferberg, 1967.

Hilberseimer, Ludwig. *Gross-Stadt Architektur.* Stuttgart: Hoffmann, ca. 1927.

Hirschbach, Frank D., et al. *Germany in the Twenties: the Artist as Social Critic.* Minneapolis: University of Minnesota, 1980.

Hofmeister, Burkhard. *Berlin: eine geographische Strukturanalyse der zwölf westlichen Bezirke.* Darmstadt: Wissenschaftliche Buchgesellschaft, 1975.

Huse, Norbert. *"Neues Bauen" 1918 bis 1933: moderne Architektur in der Weimarer Republik.* Munich: Heinz Moos, 1975.

Jahn, Max. "Architektur und Sozialismus." *BG,* VIII (1926), 809–10.

Johannes, Heinz. *Neues Bauen in Berlin.* Berlin: Deutscher Kunstverlag, 1931.

Lane, Barbara Miller. *Architecture and Politics in Germany, 1918–1945.* Cambridge: Harvard University Press, 1968.

Laquer, Walter. *Weimar: a Cultural History.* New York: Putnam, 1974.

Lindahl, Goren. "Von der Zukunftskathedrale bis zur Wohnmaschine." *Idea and Form,* n.s. 1 (1957), 226–82.

Mebes, Paul. *Um 1800.* Edited by Walter Curt Behrendt. 3rd ed. Munich: F. Bruckmann, 1920.

*Meyers Lexikon.* 7th ed. 15 vols. Leipzig: Bibliographisches Institut, 1924–33.

Müller-Wulckow, Walter. *Deutsche Baukunst der Gegenwart.* Königstein im Taunus: Langewiesche, 1929.

Novy, Klaus. *Genossenschafts-Bewegung: zur Geschichte und Zukunft der Wohnreform.* Berlin: Transit, 1983.

Novy, Klaus. *Häuserkämpfe, 1872, 1920, 1945, 1982.* Berlin: Transit, 1981.

Novy, Klaus, et al. *Stadtbauwelt 75* (24 September 1982). Issue devoted to *Baugenossenschaften.*

Platz, Gustav Adolf. *Baukunst der Neuesten Zeit.* Berlin: Propyläen-Verlag, 1927.

Rave, Rolf, and Hans-Joachim Knöfel. *Bauen seit 1900 in Berlin.* Berlin: Kiepert, 1968.

Rosenstock, Eugen. *Werkstattaussiedlung: untersuchungen über den Lebensraum des Industriearbeiters.* Berlin: Julius Springer, 1922.

Roters, Eberhard et al. *Berlin 1910–1933.* New York: Rizzoli, 1982.

Scheffler, Karl. *Berlin: Wandlungen einer Stadt.* Berlin: Bruno Cassirer, 1931.

Schinz, Alfred. *Berlin, Stadtschicksal und Städtebau.* Braunschweig: Westermann, 1964.

Schulze, Hugo, and Dallmann, Alfred. "Die Gründung der Baugenossenschaften." *50 Jahre Kampf gegen die Mietskaserne,* 4.

Schumacher, Fritz. *Strömungen in Deutscher Baukunst seit 1800.* Leipzig: E.A. Seemann, 1935.

Siedler, Eduard Jobst. *Die Lehre vom Neuen Bauen: Ein Handbuch der Baustoffe und Bauweisen.* Berlin: Bauwelt, 1932.

Stübben, Joseph and Others. *Hundert Jahre Architekten—Verein zu Berlin, 1824–1924.* Berlin: Wilhelm Ernst und Sohn, 1924.

Tafuri, Manfredo. *Architecture and Utopia: Design and Capitalist Development.* Cambridge: The MIT Press, 1976.

Tarnow, Reinhold. "Gewerkschaft und Wohnungsbau." Wand ersleb, *Handwörterbuch des Städtebaues, Wohnungs- und Siedlungswesen,* 716–19.

Taut, Bruno. "Alte Bauweisen in neuzeitlicher Form." *VW,* 1 (1919), 69–70.

Taut, Bruno. *Frühlicht: eine Folge für die Verwirklichung des neuen Baugedankens.* Reprint, Berlin: Ullstein, 1963.

*Tendenzen der zwanziger Jahre: 15. Europäische Kunstaustellung Berlin 1977* (exhibition catalog). Berlin: Dietrich Reimer, 1977.

Tucholsky, Kurt. *Deutschland, Deutschland über Alles.* Berlin: Neuer Deutscher Verlag, 1929. English translation under the German title: Amherst: University of Massachusetts, 1972.

Ungers, Liselotte. *Die Suche nach einer neuen Wohnform: Siedlungen der zwanziger Jahre damals und heute.* Stuttgart: Deutsche Verlags-Anstalt, 1983.

*Von der futuristischen zur funktionellen Stadt: Planen und Bauen in Europa 1913–1933* (exhibition catalog: part two of *Tendenzen der Zwanziger Jahre,* but also printed separately). Berlin: Dietrich Reimer, 1977.

Wagner, Martin, ed. *Das neue Berlin.* Periodical, published one year only. Berlin, 1929.

Wagner, Martin. "Die Sozialisierung der Baubetriebe." *VW,* 1 (1919), 153–56.

Wandersleb, Hermann, and Others. *Handwörterbuch des Städtebauens, Wohnungs- und Siedlungswesens.* 3 vols. Stuttgart: Kohlhammer, 1959.

*Wasmuths Lexikon der Baukunst.* 5 vols. Berlin: Ernst Wasmuth A.G., 1929–37.

Weiss, Albert. *Können die in den heutigen grossstädtischer Wohnverhältnissen liegenden Mängel und Schäden behoben werden?* Berlin: Heymann, 1912.

Weiss, Gerhard, and Christiane C. Collins. *Design for Urban Living: Germany in the 1920s.* Minneapolis: University of Minnesota, 1981.

*Wem gehört die Welt?: Kunst und Gesellschaft in der Weimarer Republik.* Berlin: Neue Gesellschaft für Bildende Kunst, 1977.

Wiedenhoeft, Ronald. "Workers' Housing as Social Politics," in *Culture and the Social Vision.* Cambridge: The Graduate School of Fine Arts, University of Pennsylvania, and the MIT Press, 1980.

Willett, John. *Art & Politics in the Weimar Period: the New Sobriety, 1917-1933.* New York: Pantheon, 1978.

Willett, John. *The Weimar Years: a Culture Cut Short.* New York: Abbeville, 1984.

Wingler, Hans M. *The Bauhaus: Weimar, Dessau, Berlin, Chicago.* Cambridge: The MIT Press, 1969.

*Zehn Jahre deutsche Geschichte: 1918-1928.* Berlin: Otto Stollberg, 1928.

**City Planning**

Albrecht, Gerhard. "Gartenstadtbewegung." *Handwörterbuch,* 262–66.

"Ansiedlungsverein Gross-Berlin." *Im Kampfe um Gross-Berlin.* Berlin: Fortschritt, 1911.

Baumeister, Reinhard. "Gemeinwohl und Sondernützen im Städtebau." *StBV,* VIII (1918), No. 4.

Baumeister, Reinhard. "Grundsätze für Stadterweiterungen." *DB,* VIII (1874), 337–46.

Behrendt, Walter Curt. *Die einheitliche Blockfront als Raumelement im Stadtbau.* Berlin: Ernst Cassirer, 1911.

"Bodenreform." *Meyers Lexikon.* 7th ed., 571–73.

Böss, Gustav. "Die Verwaltungsgemeinde Berlin und Ihre Aufgaben," Elsas, *Die Deutschen Städte, ihre Arbeit von 1918 bis 1928,* 6–8.

Brinckmann, Albert Erich. *Stadtbaukunst, geschichtliche Querschnitte und neuzeitliche Ziele.* Berlin-Neubabelsberg: Athenaion, 1920.

Brix, Josef. "Aus der Geschichte des Städtebaues in den letzten 100 Jahren." *StBV,* IV (1912).

Brix, Josef, and Felix Genzmer, eds. *Städtebauliche Vorträge aus dem Seminar für Städtebau an der königlichen technischen Hochschule zu Berlin.* 9 vols. Berlin: Wilhelm Ernst und Sohn, 1908–20.

Collins, George R., and Christiane C. Collins. *Camillo Sitte and the Birth of Modern City Planning.* New York: Random House, 1965.

Damaschke, Adolf. *Die Bodenreform.* 7th ed. Jena: Gustav Fischer, 1912.

Eberstadt, Rudolph, Bruno Möhring, and Richard Peterson. *Gross-Berlin: Ein Programm für die Planung der neuzeitlichen Gross-Stadt.* Berlin: Wasmuth, 1910.

Ehlgötz, Hermann, and Bruno Schwan. "Deutschland: Städtebau, Wohnungswesen." Schwan, *Städtebau und Wohnungswesen der Welt,* 113–41.

Ehlgötz, Hermann. "Geschichte des Städtebaues." Albrecht, *Handwörterbuch,* 288–93.

Ehrlich, Heinz. *Die Berliner Bauordnungen, Ihre Wichtigsten Bauvorschriften und Daren Einfluss auf den Wohnungsbau der Stadt Berlin.* Dr. Ing. dissertation, Berlin, 1932. Jena: Neuenhan, 1933.

Gurlitt, Cornelius. *Handbuch des Städtebaues.* Berlin: Zirkel, 1920.

Hartog, Rudolf. *Stadterweiterungen im 19. Jahrhundert.* Stuttgart: Kohlhammer, 1962.

Hegemann, Werner. *Der Städtebau nach den Ergebnissen der allgemeinen Städtebau-Ausstellung in Berlin, 1910.* 2 vols. Berlin: Wasmuth, 1911, 13.

Hegemann, Werner. *Das steinerne Berlin: Geschichte der grössten Mietskasernen-Stadt der Welt.* Berlin: Kiepenheuer, 1930. Reprinted, Berlin: Ullstein, 1963.

Heilig, Wilhelm. *Stadt- und Landbaukunde.* Berlin: Alfred Metzner Verlag, 1935.

Heiligenthal, Roman. *Deutscher Städtebau, ein Handbuch.* Heidelberg: K. Winter, 1921.

Kampffmeyer, Hans. *Die Gartenstadtbewegung.* 2nd ed. Leipzig: Berlin: Teubner, 1913.

Salomon, Hermann. "Gartenstädte." *StBV*, VI (1913).

Schwan, Bruno. *Städtebau und Wohnungswesen der Welt.* Berlin: Wasmuth, 1935.

Sitte, Camillo. *Der Städte-Bau nach seinen künstlerischen Grundsätzen.* Vienna: Carl Graeser, 1869.

Stübben, Joseph. *Der Städtebau.* 9th half-volume of Part IV of *Handbuch der Architektur.* 3rd ed. Leipzig: J.M. Gebhardt's Verlag, 1924.

Stübben, Joseph. "Städtebau von Heute." *Hundert Jahre Architekten-Verein zu Berlin, 1824–1924,* 61–63.

Taut, Bruno. *Die Auflösung der Städte.* Hagen: Folkwang 1920.

Taut, Bruno. *Die Stadtkrone.* Jena: Eugen Diederichs, 1919.

Unwin, Raymond. *Grundlagen des Städtebaues.* Translated by L. MacLean. Berlin: Baumgärtel, 1910.

"Vereinigung Berliner Architekten und Architektenverein zu Berlin." *Anregungen zur Erlangung eines Grundplanes für die städtebauliche Entwicklung von Gross-Berlin.* Berlin: Wasmuth, 1907.

Wagner, Martin. *Städtische Freiflächenpolitik.* Berlin: Heymann, 1915.

Wolf, Paul. *Städtebau: Das Formproblem der Stadt in Vergangenheit und Zukunft.* Leipzig: Klinkhardt & Biermann, 1919.

## Housing

Adler, Leo. *Neuzeitliche Miethäuser und Siedlungen.* Berlin: Ernst Pollak Verlag, 1931.

Albrecht, Gerhard, and Others. *Handwörterbuch des Wohnungswesens.* Jena: Gustav Fischer, 1930.

Bauer, Catherine. *Modern Housing.* Boston, New York: Houghton, Mifflin, 1934.

Baumeister, Reinhard. "Bauordnung und Wohnungsfrage." *StBV*, IV (1911), No. 3.

Bechly, Hans, et al. *16,000 Wohnungen für Angestellte.* Berlin: Wasmuth, 1928.

Behne, Adolf. *Neues Wohnen, neues Bauen.* Leipzig: Hesse & Becker, 1927.

Behrens, Peter, and de Fries, Heinrich. *Vom sparsamen Bauen: ein Beitrag zur Siedlungsfrage.* Berlin: Bauwelt, 1918.

Beuster, Fritz; Leyser, Erich; and Jakob Schallenberger. *Wohnungspolitik von Gestern und Morgen.* Berlin: Gross-Berliner Verein für Kleinwohnungswesen, 1931.

Block, Fritz, et al. *Probleme des Bauens: Der Wohnbau.* Potsdam: Müller & Kiepenheuer, 1928.

Blumenthal, Yvonne. *Germany: The Economic Aspects of Low Cost Housing.* New York: Housing Studies Guild, 1934.

Breitenbach, Paul von. "Runderlass betreffend Förderung von Kleinhaussiedlungen und Kleinhausbauten…" *CBB*, Vol. 37 (1917), 201–4.

Brenner, Anton. "Neuzeitliche Grundrisslösungen auf kleinstem Raum." Block, *Probleme des Bauens; Der Wohnbau,* 146–63.

Eberstadt, Rudolf. *Handbuch des Wohnungswesens und der Wohnungsfrage.* 4th ed. Jena: Gustav Fischer, 1920.

"Das Ergebnis des Bauwelt-Wettbewerbs." *BW*, XV (1924), 263–64.

de Fries, Heinrich, and Behrens, Peter. *Vom sparsamen Bauen: ein Beitrag zur Siedlungsfrage.* Berlin: Bauwelt, 1918.

*GAGFAH 1918–1968: eine Dokumentation.* Hamburg: Hammonia, 1968.

Gemeinnützige Heimstätten-Aktiengesellschaft. *GEHAG, 1924–1957: Entstehung eines gewerkschaftlichen Wohnungsunternehmens.* Berlin: GEHAG, 1957.

"Gewerkschaften und Wohnungsbau." Wandersleb, *Handwörterbuch des Städtebaues, Wohnungs- und Siedlungswesens,* II, 716–19.

Giedion, Sigfried. "Die Internationalen Kongresse für neues Bauen." Internationale Kongresse für meues Bauen und städtisches Hochbauamt in Frankfurt am Main. *Die Wohnung für das Existenzminimum,* 5–9.

Gropius, Walter. "Der Berliner Wohnungsbau." *BW,* XIX (1928), 1149–51.

Gropius, Walter. "Das Ergebnis des Reichsforschungs—Wettbewerbes." *BW,* XX (1929), 158–62.

Gropius, Walter. "Die soziologischen Grundlagen der Minimalwohnung für die städtische Bevölkerung." Internationale Kongresse für neues Bauen und städtisches Hochbauamt in Frankfurt am Main. *Die Wohnung für das Existenzminimum,* 17–19.

Gut, Albert. "Das Wohnungswesen in Deutschland seit dem Weltkriege." Stübben, *Hundert Jahre Architekten—Verein zu Berlin,* 63–77.

Gut, Albert. "Schlafstellenwesen." Albrecht, *Handwörterbuch,* 624–28.

Gut, Albert, and Others. *Der Wohnungsneubau in Deutschland nach dem Weltkriege.* Munich: F. Bruckmann, 1928.

Gutkind, Erwin, and Others. *Neues Bauen: Grundlagen zur praktischen Siedlungstätigkeit.* Berlin: Bauwelt, 1919.

Hegemann, Werner. "Schmitthenner, Bruno Taut, usw.: Sklaven eines falsch verstandenen Klassizismus?" *WMB,* XII(1928), 345–48.

Hilberseimer, Ludwig. "Die Wohnung unserer Zeit." *Form,* VI(1931), 249–70.

Hoppe, Arno. *Die Finanzierung des Wohnungsbaues und die Wohnungswirtschaft der Zukunft.* Berlin: Heymann, 1924.

Horsfall, Thomas C. *The Improvement of the Dwellings and Surroundings of the People: the Example of Germany.* Manchester: University Press, 1904.

Internationale Kongresse für neues Bauen und städtisches Hochbauamt in Frankfurt am Main. *Die Wohnung für das Existenzminimum.* Frankfurt: Englert & Schlosser, 1930.

Internationaler Verband für Wohnungswesen. *Die sozialpolitische Bedeutung der Wohnungswirtschaft in Gegenwart und Zukunft.* Frankfurt/Main: Internationaler Verband für Wohnungswesen, 1931.

Jobst, Gerhard. *Kleinwohnungsbau in Holland.* Berlin: Wilhelm Ernst & Sohn, 1922.

Klein, Alexander. "Beiträge zur Wohnungsfrage." Block, *Probleme des Bauens: der Wohnbau,* 116–45.

Luckhardt, Hans; Luckhardt, Wassili; and Anker, Alfons. "Versuche zur fortentwicklung des Wohnbaues." *BW,* XVII (1927), 1215–18.

von Mangoldt, Rose. "Wohnungsreform." *WLB,* V, 618–20.

May, Ernst, and Gropius, Walter. "Flachbau-Hochbau." *Form,* IV(1929), 672.

May, Ernst. "Die Wohnung für das Existenzminimum." Internationale Kongresse für neues Bauen und städtisches Hochbauamt in Frankfurt am Main, *Die Wohnung für das Existenzminimum,* 10–16.

Schallenberger, Jakob, and Kraffert, Hans. *Berliner Wohnungsbauten aus öffentlichen Mitteln.* Berlin: Bauwelt, 1926.

Schallenberger, Jakob. *Der Wohnungsneubau in Berlin.* Berlin: Berliner Wohnungsfürsorge-gesellschaft, n.d.

Schaukal, Richard von. *Die Mietwohnung, eine Kulturfrage.* 3rd ed. Munich: G. Müller, 1911.

Schinz, Alfred. "Das mehrgeschossige Miethaus." Berlin, Taipei, 1967. (Typescript)

Schmidt, Friedrich, and Ebel, Martin. *Wohnungsbau der Nachkriegszeit in Deutschland.* Berlin: Eulen Verlag, n.d.

Schmitthenner, Paul. *Das deutsche Wohnhaus.* Stuttgart: K. Wittwer, 1932.

Schulze, Hugo, and Dallmann, Alfred. *50 Jahre Kampf gegen die Mietskaserne.* Berlin: Baugenossenschaft Freie Scholle, 1947.

Schwan, Bruno. *Wohnungsnot und Wohnungselend in Deutschland.* Berlin: Deutscher Verein für Wohnungsreform, 1929.

Schwan, Bruno. "Wohnungsreform." Albrecht, *Handwörterbuch,* 836–38.

Siedler, Eduard Jobst. "Heimstättengärten in der Gross-stadt." Block, *Probleme des Bauens; Der Wohnbau,* 47–54.

*Soziale Bauwirtschaft* (periodical).

Spörhase, Rolf. "Wohnungsunternehmung im rahmen Staatlicher Wohnungspolitik." *Wohnungsunternehmungen im Wandel der Zeit*, 88–90.

Spörhase, Rolf. *Wohnungsunternehmungen im Wandel der Zeit.* Hamburg: Br. Sachse, 1947.

Taut, Bruno. *Bauen: der neue Wohnbau.* Leipzig, Berlin: Klinkhardt & Biermann, 1927.

Taut, Bruno. "Die Erde eine gute Wohnung." *VW*, I (1919), 45.

Taut, Bruno. "Ein Ledigenheim in Schöneberg." *StBK*, I(1920), 136–138.

Taut, Bruno. *Die neue Wohnung: die Frau als Schöpferin.* 5th ed., rev. Leipzig: Klinkhardt & Biermann, 1928.

Taut, Bruno. *Ein Wohnhaus.* Stuttgart: Franckh'sche Verlagshandlung W. Keller, 1927.

*40 Jahre Berlinische Bodengesellschaft.* Berlin: Privately Printed, 1930.

*40 Jahre Gemeinnützige Heimstätten-Baugesellschaft der BVG GmbH.* Berlin: Privately Printed, 1964.

Wächter, Klaus. *Wohnen in der stadtischen Agglomeration des zwanzigsten Jahrhunderts.* Stuttgart: Karl Kramer, 1971.

Wagner, Martin. "Aufgaben im Berliner Wohnungsbau." *BW*, XIX (1928), 1129–31.

*Wohnungswirtschaft* (periodical).

Wolf, Paul. *Wohnung und Siedlung.* Berlin: Wasmuth, 1926.

Wolz, Otto. "Parlament und Wohnungsfrage." Albrecht, *Handwörterbuch*, 583–88.

Wutzky, Emil. "Wohnungswirtschaft." Elsas, *Die Deutschen Städte, ihre Arbeit von 1918 vis 1928*, 58–62.

Zimmermann, Waldemar. "Kulturliche und soziale Bedeutung des Wohnwesens und seine Wechselbeziehung zur Sozialpolitik." Albrecht, *Handwörterbuch*, 451–59.

## Individual Artists and Architects

*Breuer*

Breuer, Marcel. "Beiträge zur Frage des Hochhauses." *Form*, V(1930), 113–17.

*Damaschke*

Tetzner, Eike. "Adolf Damaschke." Akademie fur Raumforschung und Landesplanung. *Handwörterbuch der Raumforschung und Landesplanung*, 279.

*Forbat*

Forbat, Fred. "Profile: Fred Forbat." *Der Aufbau*, Vol. 12 (1957), 247–48.

*Gropius*

Argan, Giulio Carlo. *Gropius und das Bauhaus.* Reinbeck bei Hamburg: Rowohlt, 1962.

Fitch, James Marston. *Walter Gropius.* New York: Braziller, 1960.

Franciscono, Marcel. *Walter Gropius and the Foundation of the Bauhaus in Weimar.* Urbana: University of Illinois, 1971.

Gropius, Walter. "Profile: Walter Gropius." *Der Aufbau*, Vol. 12(1957), 25–27.

*Häring*

Lauterbach, Heinrich, and Jödicke, Jürgen. *Hugo Häring: Schriften, Entwurfe, Bauten.* Stuttgart: Karl Krämer, 1965.

*Henning*

Henning, P.R. "Keramik und Baukunst." *Form,* I(1926), 76–78.

*Hilberseimer*

Hilberseimer, Ludwig. "Profile: Ludwig K. Hilberseimer." *Der Aufbau,* Vol. 14(1959), 107–10.

*Klein*

Klein, Alexander. "Profile: Alexander Klein." *Der Aufbau,* Vol. 14(1959), 504–6.

*Krämer*

Osborn, Max. *Jean Krämer.* Berlin: Friedrich Ernst Hübsch, 1927.

*Lassen*

"Professor Architekt Heinz Lassen 60 Jahre alt." *BW,* XV(1924), 250.

*Luckhardt*

Kultermann, Udo. *Wassili und Hans Luckhardt: Bauten und Entwürfe.* Tübingen: Wasmuth, 1958.
Wiedenhoeft, Ronald V. *Hans and Wassili Luckhardt: a Metamorphosis in Modern German Architecture.* Unpublished Master's Thesis, University of Wisconsin, 1964.

*Mebes*

Meyer, Edina. *Paul Mebes: Miethausbau in Berlin 1906–38.* Berlin: Richard Seitz, 1972.

*Salvisberg*

Westheim, Paul. *Neuere Arbeiten von O.R. Salvisberg.* Berlin: Friedrich Ernst Hübsch, 1927.

*Scharoun*

"Martin Wagner gewinnt Scharoun." *WMB,* XII(1929), 84.
Pfannkuch, Peter, and Heinrich Lauterbach. *Hans Scharoun.* Berlin: Akademie der Künste, 1967.

*Straumer*

Stahl, Fritz. *Heinrich Straumer.* Berlin: Friedrich Ernst Hübsch, 1927.

*Taut*

Akademie der Künste. *Bruno Taut 1880–1938.* Berlin: Akademie der Künste, 1980.
Junghans, Kurt. *Bruno Taut 1880–1938.* Berlin: Henschelverlag, 1970.
Whyte, Ian Boyd. *Bruno Taut and the Architecture of Activism.* Cambridge: Cambridge University, 1982.

*Wagner*

Haberland, Georg. "Offener Brief an Herrn Dr. Ing. Martin Wagner." *VW*, I(1919), 312–13.
Kempmann, Jochen. *Das Ideengut Martin Wagners als Beispiel für die Entwicklung der städtebaulichen Gedankengänge seit 1900*. Dr. Ing. dissertation, *Technische Universität*, Berlin, 1968.
Scarpa, Ludovica. *Martin Wagner e Berlino: casa e città nella Republica di Weimar 1918–1933*. Rome: Officina, 1983.
Wagner, Martin. "Offener Brief an Herrn Kommerzienrat Haberland." *VW*, I(1919), 285–86.
Wagner, Martin. "Regie." *BW*, XXI(1930), 801–2.

*Wolf*

"Stadtbaurat Wolf 50 Jahre alt." *BW*, XX(1929), 1174.

**Specific *Siedlungen* or *Wohnbauten***

Adler, Leo. "Siedlungen in Berlin-Britz." *WMB*, XI (1927), 385–90.
*Die Bauwerke und Kunstdenkmäler von Berlin: Bezirk Zehlendorf, Siedlung Onkel Tom, Einfamilienreihenhäuser 1929, Architekt Bruno Taut*. Berlin: Gebr. Mann, 1980.
Behne, Adolf. "Die Zehlendorfer Siedlung der GEHAG." *Form*, IV (1929), 4–8.
Dietrich, Ulf. "Neuer Betriebsbahnhof und Wohnbauten der Berliner Strassenbahn." *WMB*, XIV (1930), 577–82.
"Erwin Gutkind: Wohnhausblock in Berlin-Lichtenberg." *BW*, XIX (1928), Heft 2.
"Die feuer- und rauchlose Siedlung in Berlin-Steglitz." *WMB*, XVI (1932), 115–22.
"Die Friedrich Ebert Siedlung in Berlin." *WMB*, XVI (1932), 429–35.
"GEHAG Gross-Siedlung Karl Legien Stadt an der Carmen Sylva Strasse." *BW*, XXII (1931), Heft 19.
Gorgas, Curt. "Gross-Siedlung Siemensstadt, Berlin." *BW*, XXI (1930), Heft 46.
"Gross-Siedlung Berlin-Reinickendorf, Schiller Promenade." *BW*, XXI (1930), Heft 48.
"Gross-Siedlung Siemensstadt—Bebauung am Goebelplatz und am Geislerpfad—1930–31." *BW*, XXII (1931), Heft 47.
"Gross-Stadt Siedlung: Eine neue Lösung des Reihenhaus—Probleme." *BW*, XVII (1926), Heft 12.
Hegemann, Werner. "Dachüberstand, Frostschäden und Kritik der 'Rationalen Vernunft' Bruno Tauts." *WMB*, XI (1927), 463.
Hegemann, Werner. "Randbebauung des Tempelhofer Feldes." *WMB*, IX (1925), 205–8.
Hegemann, Werner. "Wohnhausgruppe der GAGFAH, Gemeinnützigen A.G. für Angestellten-Heimstätten, Berlin, in Lichterfelde." *WMB*, XI (1927), 425–29.
Hertlein, Hans. *Siemensbauten*. Berlin: Ernst Wasmuth A.G. n.d.
"Kinderheim im Miethausblock." *BW*, XIX (1928), Heft 38.
Lehwess, Walter. "Kleinhaussiedlung in Berlin-Dahlem." *StBK*, II (1921), 213–20.
Lotz, Wilhelm. "Die GAGFAH-Siedlung." *Form*, III (1928), 289–98.
Mebes, Paul. "Die feuer- und rauchlose Siedlung in Berlin-Steglitz." *WMB*, XVI (1932), 115–22.
Mebes, Paul. "Die Friedrich Ebert Siedlung in Berlin." *WMB*, XVI (1932), 429–35.
"Neue Wohnhausgruppe der Architekten Paul Mebes und Paul Emmerich, Berlin." *NB*, IX (1927), 1–2.
"Die Neubauten der Siedlung 'Heimat' in Berlin-Siemensstadt." *WMB*, XVI (1932), 512–13.
"Neue Bauten der Siedlung Siemensstadt." *WMB*, XIV (1930), 186–88.
Schwab, Alexander. "Zur GEHAG-Siedlung Zehlendorf: Grundsätzliches und Wirtschaftliches." *Form*, IV (1929), 8–14.

Siedler, Eduard Jobst. "Ein Gross-Siedlungsvorhaben in Zehlendorf." *BG,* VII (1926), 965ff.

"Siedlung Heimat in Berlin-Siemensstadt." *WMB,* XIV (1930), 537–41.

Stahl, Fritz. "Die Gartenstadt Staaken." *WMB,* III (1918/19), 137–98.

Stein, Georg. "Neue Strasenbahnersiedlung mit Betriebsbahnhof in der Müllerstrasse, Berlin N." *NB,* IX (1927), 261–64.

"1000 Wohnungen: Siedlung in Britz." *BW,* XVIII (1927), Heft 9.

Taut, Bruno, Jakob Schallenberger, and Hans Kraffert. "Erklärungen zur Siedlung der GEHAG in Zehlendorf." *BG,* VII (1926), 1017–18.

"Das Tempelhofer Feld." *VW,* II (1920), 202–3.

# Index